Remembrances of Arnold Wm. Rachman

This book explores the implications of Arnold Rachman's work in interpreting and applying Sándor Ferenczi's approach to psychoanalysis to contemporary psychoanalytic theory and practice.

Drawing on contributions from colleagues, analysands, and supervisees, this book allows us to see how, through Rachman's work, the ideas that Ferenczi had have been amplified and used as a base for a clear approach to psychoanalytic work. In doing so, he has allowed Ferenczi's work to go from being a forgotten part of psychoanalytic history to being an influential figure in psychoanalysis today, especially in the United States and in Europe.

With fascinating insights on the place of Ferenczi and Rachman's work in contemporary psychoanalytic theory and practice, this book is key reading for psychoanalysts, psychotherapists, and historians of thought.

Harold Kooden, PhD, is a Fellow of the American Psychological Association (APA), the founder and board member of the National Gay and Lesbian Health Education Foundation, and a founding member and community activist of Services and Advocacy for GLBT Elders (SAGE) and the NYC AIDS Network.

Michael Larivière is a psychoanalyst, in private practice in Strasbourg, France, where he moved after a childhood and adolescence spent between New York, Miami, and Montreal. He is a former Associate Professor of Psychiatry at the Faculty of Medicine of Strasbourg University. He is the author of five books.

Evolutions in Psychoanalysis Book Series
Daniel Goldin and Melvin Bronstein
Series Editors

Under the editorship of Melvin Bronstein and Daniel Goldin, the Evolutions in Psychoanalysis book series provides a shared space for writers who are eager to revisit formative psychoanalytical ideas in often innovative new ways. The word 'evolve' literally means 'to unroll', and the contemporary use of the latter term suggests that something new can be revealed through a process of incremental unravelling. As a definition of both the aspirations of this series and of psychoanalysis itself, this understanding exemplifies the possibility that one can take apart by creating and create by taking apart.

The volumes in this series do not represent a particular school of psychoanalytic thought, but rather comprise and encourage new voices from all schools and spaces – across time and geographical location – in the knowledge that brilliant thinkers and ideas can emerge from unforeseen places. The series does also encompass the editors' interests in how contemporary psychoanalysis intersects with society and culture at large; differing analyses of the micro-processes that take place in clinical encounters; and the influence of other disciplines – such as philosophy and infant-research – upon the field of psychoanalysis, and welcomes contributions to these and other topics.

Of critical importance to the formation of this series is its aspiration to foreground voices from marginalized ethnic groups, for the vitality and creativity they offer which is so necessary to the field, and to continue in the direction of redress and repair for the omissions and exclusions of the past.

Remembrances of Arnold Wm. Rachman
Sándor Ferenczi Scholar and Psychoanalyst
Harold Kooden and Michael Larivière

Psychoanalysis Through the Lens of Narcissism
Orna Afek

Practicing Psychoanalysis in Israel: Seeing Through Blindness
Gabriela Mann

For more information about this series, please visit: https://www.routledge.com/Evolutions-in-Psychoanalysis-Book-Series/book-series/EVIPS

Remembrances of Arnold Wm. Rachman

Sándor Ferenczi Scholar and Psychoanalyst

Edited by Harold Kooden, Senior Editor and Michael Larivière, Editor

Routledge
Taylor & Francis Group

LONDON AND NEW YORK

Designed cover image: © Nancy Rachman

First published 2026
by Routledge
4 Park Square, Milton Park, Abingdon, Oxon OX14 4RN

and by Routledge
605 Third Avenue, New York, NY 10158

Routledge is an imprint of the Taylor & Francis Group, an informa business

British Library Cataloguing-in-Publication Data
A catalogue record for this book is available from the British Library

ISBN: 978-1-032-48844-8 (hbk)
ISBN: 978-1-032-48845-5 (pbk)
ISBN: 978-1-003-39108-1 (ebk)

DOI: 10.4324/9781003391081

Typeset in Optima
by SPi Technologies India Pvt Ltd (Straive)

Contents

Contributors

Fergal Brady is President of the Irish Psycho-Analytical Association. He met Arnold in 2017 at a psychiatric conference in Florence, Italy. There was an immediate connection as Fergal was very warm and friendly as well as being very interested in Sándor Ferenczi. He expressed his desire to collaborate on future projects, such as the Irish history and the meaning of the Irish perspective on psychoanalysis.

Jill Choder-Goldman was an analytic trainee at the Postgraduate Center for Mental Health and chose Arnold as her supervisor. It was through this relationship that she developed an interest in Ferenczi as there never was a mention of Ferenczi in the formal training at the Center. Since then, she has become a creative and flexible psychoanalyst.

Ann D'Ercole is a distinguished professor of psychoanalysis at the William Alanson White Institute in New York City. She initially contacted Arnold when she was writing a biography on Clara Thompson, one of the founders of Interpersonal Psychology. She and Arnold collaborated on an article on Clara Thompson who was an analysand of Ferenczi. She became a dear friend as well as colleague.

Mark Feldman was a former patient of Arnold's who started seeing him when he was a child. He claims Arnold's therapeutic influence changed his entire life.

Alan Fishman was a former analysand of Arnold's who considers his analysis as one of the significant influences in his life.

Henry Kellerman was one of a trio of colleagues/friends, along with Robert J. Marshall, PhD, who studied with Arnold at the Postgraduate Center for Mental Health. Though they had different frames of reference within psychoanalysis, they respected each other's perspective which prevented them from strictly adhering to an orthodoxy within the field. They were close friends for over fifty years.

Robert E. Kennedy is a Jesuit priest who specifically wanted a Jewish analyst when he entered psychoanalysis. He chose Arnold as his analyst. He is also a sensei in a traditional Japanese order. He has successfully combined his Catholic thinking with his being an honor teacher in this Japanese order. Post analysis, Kennedy and Arnold remained close colleagues and friends.

Susan A. Klett was a colleague from the Postgraduate Center who became a dear friend. Since she and Arnold were both highly interested in the relationship between trauma and sexual abuse, they collaborated on the book, *Analysis of Incest Trauma* which was published in 2015.

Harold Kooden and Arnold were in the same graduate program at the University of Chicago and have been friends for over sixty-three years. They were the dearest of friends and considered each other brothers. The collegial relationship incorporated weekly mutual-analysis and supportive work on Arnold's writings on Ferenczi. He is senior editor of this Festschrift.

Joseph Lichtenberg died in 2021. We are fortunate that he wrote and submitted his essay in the years prior. Dr. Lichtenberg had a long productive career as a psychoanalyst and wrote numerous books, chapters, and articles on topics as varied as infant research, ego psychology, self-psychology, his Motivational Systems Theory, as well as principles of psychoanalytic techniques. He was also editor-in-chief of Psychoanalytic Inquiry, a psychoanalytic journal and of Psychoanalytic Inquiry Book Series. His personal analyst was an analysand of Ferenczi. He had both an intellectual and interpersonal connection with Arnold.

Robert J. Marshall is one of a trio of colleagues/friends along with Henry Kellerman, PhD, who studied with Arnold at the Postgraduate Center. Though Dr. Marshall has a very different psychoanalytic perspective, he had been consistently respectful of his and Arnold's differences. He was a very important part of Arnold's professional and personal life for over fifty years.

Paul Mattick is a philosopher who became interested in psychoanalysis. He has collaborated with Arnold and written articles and a book demonstrating his integration between psychoanalysis and culture resulting in a philosophical understanding of human behavior.

Judit Mészáros is considered one of the world's most important scholars on the international organizations devoted to Sándor Ferenczi. As a Hungarian psychoanalyst, she has become an international ambassador from the Budapest School of Psychoanalysis. She and Arnold were friends and colleagues for over thirty years.

Jeffrey Moussaieff Masson became world-famous for his 1984 book, *The Assault on Truth*, for which he was ostracized from the psychoanalytic world for his exposé on Freud. He was former head of the Freud Archives where he had access to all of Freud's letters thus presenting a documented dissident perspective in psychoanalysis. He has praised Arnold's work on Ferenczi as further evidence of significant changes in psychoanalytic thinking.

Clara Mucci University of Bergamo, Italy met Arnold in a seminar on Ferenczi at a conference on trauma in Florence, Italy. She is focused on integrating Ferenczi's concepts on trauma with contemporary neurological research on trauma. She and Arnold collaborated on the book, *Ferenczi's Confusion of Tongues Theory of Trauma: A Relational Neurobiological Perspective* which was published in 2024.

Salvador Rocha Pineda resides in Mexico and is a physician and psychoanalyst. He has been a consultant for 30 years in the National Institute of Medical Sciences and Nutrition Salvador Zubirán in the areas related to Anorexia and Bulimia and Liaison Psychiatry. He has also published and presented on the field of intersections of art, literature, the body, philosophy and psychoanalysis. Dr. Pineda was a member of the Sándor Ferenczi Study Group: México, founded by Arnold Wm. Rachman and Uriel García Varela.

Robert Prince was Arnold's analysand and then, supervisee on his path to becoming a psychoanalyst. Through his interaction with Arnold, he became exposed to Ferenczi so that he has incorporated Ferenczi into his practice. He and Arnold were colleagues with a similar frame of mind.

Uriel García Varela is a young, recent colleague from Mexico who met Arnold in 2023 at an international conference celebrating the 150th anniversary of Ferenczi's birth (1873). Their connection was immediate due to their shared interest in Ferenczi. Ferenczi was totally missing in his psychoanalytic training in Mexico—an absence similar to Arnold's experience in the United States. Their shared admiration for Ferenczi and their wish to incorporate Ferenczi concepts into Mexican psychoanalytic training resulted in their conducting a virtual study group in Mexico in late 2023 as well as planning for an in-person conference in Mexico City to take place at a later date.

Introduction

Harold Kooden

I was asked to be the senior editor of this Festschrift when Michael Larivière became ill and could no longer support this project. He had originated the idea of this Festschrift for Arnold Rachman which gave Arnold the impetus to request contributions from colleagues, former clients, analysands, and friends, such as me. I gladly wrote my contribution in which I covered our sixty-year history beginning in graduate school and continuing to the present day. As a non-psychoanalytic psychotherapist, I also felt that I could evaluate and comment on Arnold's work from a different perspective which emphasized the value of Arnold's work for the psychotherapeutic profession. Much of what I wrote would explain why I would be considered as senior editor when Michael became ill. I accepted becoming the role as I believed that the psychoanalytic and psychotherapeutic professional world needed to have a clear statement honoring the effects of Arnold's research and therapeutic practice.

Anyone reading this Festschrift will immediately see a difference between a European Festschrift and a U.S. one. The former is usually a collection of colleagues' research and essays stimulated by the honoree's work. It is clearly an intellectual approach to creating a Festschrift honoring the recipient. As you will see, this Festschrift contains some of these elements but also the emotional and personal impact that Arnold has had on the lives of the contributors. But there is more than a simple, historical recounting of his influence; there are also statements on the current relevance of his work as well as its future relevance for both the contributor and the field in general. This stress on the present and future is where the European and U.S. Festschrifts are similar. The former shows the influence on the present and future by the inspired research and papers stimulated by the honoree's work. The latter Festschrift has both the historically emotional and professional impact of Arnold's work on the contributor, but also how Arnold's work coincides with current research in his field and where his research can affect a future direction for younger colleagues, one of whom is a contributor.

As a way to better understand the relevance of the contribution, there will be a brief description of the relationship between Arnold and the writer. This way you will have a better idea of how Arnold's lifetime work since the 1970s has had both a national and international influence. His determination and dedication to placing Sándor Ferenczi and Elizabeth Severn in their rightful place in the evolving history of psychoanalysis is now being recognized. This Festschrift dedicated to Arnold Rachman is a reflection of this moment in time.

Foreword

Michael Larivière

One of the things that are most striking about psychoanalysts is how resistant they are to what is on offer in psychoanalysis, namely, to enable us to be curious about something other than the past, about something other than what we refer to as home. The British psychoanalyst, Adam Phillips, has written extensively about this: our resistance to dispelling nostalgia. And this resistance is what Freud was most interested in: understanding why the therapy he had invented was met with such hostility and fear. But also understanding why psychoanalysis so consistently failed to do what we think we expect of it: to free us from the pleasure of suffering, from our ambition to repeat the past, from our commitment to our own unhappiness, from our resistance to the possibility of pleasure. Freud referred to this as *Todestrieb*, the *death* instinct, a notion to this day refused by many in our profession.

These are issues that mattered a great deal to one of Freud's earliest and closest collaborators, Sándor Ferenczi. I think it can safely be said that one of the main differences between Freud and Ferenczi is that while Freud was always ambivalent about psychoanalysis as a form of therapy, Ferenczi never doubted that that was its main interest. Which is why he states in his *Clinical Diary* that Freud's inclination to keep communicating on technical points to the minimum should be seen as his blind spot, even as his resistance to his own invention. And indeed, it could be argued that Freud was afraid of the *wildness* his method might give way to. Which is probably why he said of those who recognized transference and resistance as the focal point of his method that they belonged irretrievably to the *mad horde*. And, as we know, *mad* is how Ferenczi was referred to by quite a few of Freud's early followers (Freud himself was more nuanced in his criticism). Which brings me to Arnold. For it was by that, "mad" version of psychoanalysis that his imagination was very early on captured. So much so that it became for him, in William James' words, something "to be going on from". Psychoanalysis can't not be wild, something it takes *chutzpah* to acknowledge – a quality Arnold has consistently demonstrated.

Arnold and I met roughly thirty years ago in Budapest, where we were both presenting at a Ferenczi Conference. As you may know, tourists who fly to Budapest are advised to use the small busses that are made available to take them to their respective hotels. I took the advice. Arnold was sitting with someone at the very front of the bus, myself only a few seats behind, close enough to hear him talking to that person – and recognize the New York accent I had heard throughout my childhood. That was enough for me to want to get to know this man. Chance had it that we were staying at the same hotel, and it was while waiting to be signed in at the reception desk that I first made contact. One thing very quickly led to another, and Arnold invited me to join him and other colleagues for dinner at Gundel that very evening. I gratefully accepted the invitation – and that was it. The sense of closeness that developed was such that it was as if we had always known one another.

Of course, we mostly talked about psychoanalysis during the meal. Arnold's enthusiasm, his belief that psychoanalysis can make people feel alive in ways they prefer, that it can help them actually get the lives they want, was contagious. But he further stressed that the version of psychoanalysis needed for this to have a chance of happening was not the one Freud offered but, rather, Sándor Ferenczi's. For this reason, in his work of over forty years, Arnold has sought to, as it were, recreate Ferenczi, reimagine him, fully invoke him, resurrect him, to offer life to what had virtually become a shadow. He has strived to forge a style that is capable of evoking the shivering ambiguities of what is experienced by both parties in the course of an analysis, coupling the need to show empathy with the need to be true to what psychoanalysis is like in all its variety and fullness.

His first contributions involved examining the issues of theory and technique in analytic group therapy, first and foremost with adolescents. He was one of the first group therapists in America to publish papers on the introduction of encounter and intensive group therapy, as well as non-interpretative measures in analytic group psychotherapy. He then went on to publish several books, as well as numerous articles, on Ferenczi's contribution to psychoanalysis, demonstrating that it was he, Ferenczi, and not Kohut, who had first insisted on the importance of clinical empathy in analysis. He further re-evaluated Ferenczi's introduction of non-interpretative measures as meaningful in the analysis of trauma cases.

He also contributed towards calling back to attention, in America, the work of other important analysts, such as Michael Balint and, more recently, Elizabeth Severn (and, with them, The Budapest School of Psychoanalysis), all of which will be documented throughout this book.

This is why I thought it only right that we pay tribute to him with a *Festschrift* honoring both his academic and clinical career. As Harold Kooden very rightly says, Arnold's commitment to Ferenczi is a passionate one. The main reason for this commitment, in my opinion, is that Ferenczi made it possible for him to unashamedly bring his heart into the therapeutic process, a position often seen as, if not unacceptable, certainly controversial by the so-called mainstream psychoanalysis. For it does indeed take *chutzpah* to address the very difficult question of why it is that psychoanalysis keeps on not working in the same way. This is an issue that both Freud and Ferenczi were extremely interested in: failure. How and why, so often, doesn't psychoanalysis work? An interest, as Adam Phillips puts it, in the heuristic value of anomaly and ignorance. And it is because he has always been able to address such issues that Arnold never was dogmatic in his approach of our would-be science. As we all know and often refuse to acknowledge, dogmatism is rampant in our field. A quality, or a capacity, that every analyst should show is to remain puzzled about what she or he is doing (and writing about). There should always be more conjecture and speculation about what we do, than instruction or even guidelines.

Another question that Arnold has never ceased to ask himself is: what kind of freedom does the analyst need in order to free the patient to speak? So, I will close by recalling that it was precisely because this was a question that mattered to him most that Freud had warned Ferenczi that he, Ferenczi, was "too much under the influence of his patients" (*Clinical Diary*, Harvard University Press, 1988, p. 46). I am quite sure that Arnold would disagree with me here, a disagreement I welcome as an opportunity to enrich one another analytically, intellectually, and emotionally. And I am sure Arnold would think the same.

1 My Personal Odyssey in Becoming a Ferenczian Psychoanalyst

Arnold Wm. Rachman

NOTE: Unfortunately, Arnold passed away on September 15, 2024 before he was able to complete this chapter on how he became a Ferenczi scholar and practitioner. What follows is his unfinished draft. His story includes the precursors as to why Ferenczi became so important to him, recognizing those individuals who early on made a great impact on him as a youth and those who encouraged and supported him throughout his undergraduate and graduate education and psychoanalytic training. Had he continued writing, Arnold would have described, as he so often told it, how he discovered Sándor Ferenczi on his own in the mid-1970's. Ferenczi was never mentioned in any of his formal psychoanalytic training. While doing research one day in the Postgraduate Center library, Arnold found the three volumes of Ferenczi's *Collected Papers* which he discovered had only been checked out by one other person.

Through his work, Arnold became an internationally and nationally known Ferenczi scholar. His dedication to expanding knowledge about who and what influenced Ferenczi included extensive research, writings, and presentations about Elizabeth Severn, one of Ferenczi's most famous cases. He was very proud of this work and that he was able to contribute a collection of papers and other documents about her to the Library of Congress and the Ferenczi International Center in Budapest. In 2023, at the Ferenczi 150th Anniversary International Conference in Budapest, Arnold was honored for his donation by Judit Mészáros, his longtime dear friend and colleague. With Judit's support, Arnold's contribution established the Elizabeth Severn section of the Ferenczi Archives at the center. For that and for their many productive years working together to preserve the work of Sándor Ferenczi, I know Arnold was very grateful. For Arnold, it was important that Ferenczi never be forgotten again, as he had discovered that day back in the 1970s in the Postgraduate Center Library. During this same conference, Arnold met Uriel García Varela, a psychoanalyst from Mexico who shared Arnold's same passion for Ferenczi as well as a strong desire to introduce others to Ferenczi. They developed a strong bond and fruitful working relationship. In Arnold's last year, they co-taught a virtual course with Mexican therapists and were planning to organize an in-person conference in Mexico City. Arnold took

DOI: 10.4324/9781003391081-1

great pride in the work Uriel and he were doing together knowing there would be another person to carry on Ferenczi's work.

Also, in 2023, Arnold published the book, *Psychoanalysis and Society's Neglect of the Sexual Abuse of Children, Youth and Adults: Re-addressing Freud's Original Theory of Sexual Abuse and Trauma*. For this work, Arnold was awarded the Sándor Ferenczi Award by the International Society for the Study of Trauma and Dissociation for the best published work in the realm of psychoanalysis related to trauma and dissociation in the last twenty-four months. Arnold was very honored by this recognition and took great pride in receiving the award plaque.

Arnold was a great admirer of Jeffrey Moussaieff Masson, respecting his work. They corresponded regularly in these last few years with each email exchange meaning so much to Arnold. Arnold was also very honored to be asked to contribute a chapter for a new book, *Contemporary Perspectives on Freud's Seduction Theory and Psychotherapy. Revisiting Masson's 'The Assault on Truth'*. Arnold completed what he felt was one of his most important writings and lived to see a galley of the book which was published soon after he died.

Arnold would have included all this and much more had he been able to continue this chapter on his journey to be the psychoanalyst and Ferenczi scholar that he became. Arnold loved his work, valued his many colleagues and friends in the profession and was grateful to those who took the time and care to contribute to this book.

Harold Kooden
Senior Editor

My Grandmother, Bertha Metsch Beispiel, "Granny": My Original Therapeutic Role Model

I was nine years old when my father died and my grandmother, whom we called "Granny," became an essential part of my life, my "other mother" for my sister and me. Granny was fully present in my life, which was important since my mother had to become the sole family provider. During the week, my mother held down two jobs, one in the daytime and one at night. We generally saw my mother on the weekends. She was physically present but not emotionally involved. We rarely had emotional contact, as I remember my mother as depressed, distant, and unaffectionate after my father's death. She gave the job of mothering her children to my grandmother. For some reason she did not turn to my sister or me to gain love and support during her darkest days. When I discussed my grandmother in my personal analysis, I began to think about her as a "lifesaving force." Granny was a warm, loving, responsive, and physically affectionate human being. She was my "emotional savior," calling me *meiner lieben*, "my loved one," in Yiddish. Clearly, she was a role model for having a loving, close relationship with another human being. There was more to Granny than her loving personality. She became my first role model for being a therapeutic agent.

When I was sixteen years old, another teenage member of my extended family had what would be called then a "nervous breakdown." Looking back at this disturbing incident, I have tried to organize the event in some meaningful way. On his eighteenth birthday, this male family member received a letter from the armed services to register for the draft. He became very anxious and could not continue to go to business school where he was training to work in the computer field. He became enraged at his mother, took a large knife from their kitchen, and threatened her with it. He then locked himself in his room and would not leave. My grandmother was very close to this part of the extended family. One morning, Granny paid her daily visit to the family. When the young man heard his "Auntie" was in the apartment, he summoned her by shouting from his room. To everyone's astonishment, he unlocked the door and invited her to join him. Everyone told her not to go in because he still had the knife he used to threaten his mother. Granny had the courage to listen to his thoughts and feelings, and she felt safe because of the loving relationship she had with her nephew. They were heard talking, sometimes in loud voices, but there were no angry outbursts. After about an hour, the door opened, Granny holding her nephew's hand. He was tearful as she led him to the living room couch to sit down and began to tell the family that her nephew is willing to see a doctor to help him with his problems. He was willing to talk to his auntie, but no one else. She told him he needed help with his nervousness and his anger with his mother. This demure 5'2" woman was able to quiet the demons in this eighteen-year-old who threatened to harm his mother.

With Granny virtually and symbolically holding his hand, he was able to agree to see a doctor, who referred him to the adolescent ward of a psychiatric hospital. He was a psychiatric inpatient for a year or so and then became an outpatient for several years. The recovery treatment helped him return to computer training, remaining in the workforce until he retired in his late sixties. I witnessed in that turbulent event during my adolescence, the "therapeutic presence" my grandmother demonstrated. It now has been over seventy years since that incident, yet I vividly remember it. I carry with me my Granny's tenderness, empathy, love, and responsiveness. As I, describe below the mentors in my life, it will be clear that I have always been attached to individuals, e.g. friends, teachers, supervisors, and scholars, who demonstrated these personal qualities. It is not far-fetched to say that, in Sándor Ferenczi, I saw my Granny.

University of Buffalo: Olive Lester, PhD

The dawn of my intellectual consciousness occurred at the University of Buffalo (UB) in the 1950s. I entered college with the idea that I would train to become a pediatrician; so I could be of service to others. UB was a liberal academic institution, known as the "Berkeley of the East." The head of the psychology department was Olive Lester, PhD. She graduated from UB in 1924, was the first woman to attend the College of Arts and Sciences, the first person to earn a bachelor's degree in psychology, and one of the first women in the country to head a psychology department. A social psychologist, she was also an outspoken advocate for women.

When I entered UB, my fantasy to become a pediatrician took a dramatic turn as a result of Dr. Lester who taught my first psychology course, "Introduction to Psychology." It was impressive that the chairman of the Psychology Department took the time to teach this introductory course; thus, pioneering the use of the most experienced and gifted faculty to motivate students to become interested in psychology. She brought enthusiasm, vitality, kindness, and a gentle manner to her teaching, which helped me to develop an interest in psychology. Dr. Lester, in the tradition of Ferenczi, did more than teach; she reached out to me and made an encouraging and compassionate gesture that motivated me to think about psychology as a career. She gave me an A on my final paper for the course, adding: "You should consider thinking about becoming a psychologist. You have the capacity."

University of Chicago: The Committee on Human Development

While I was studying for my Master's Degree in Psychology at Roosevelt University in Chicago, I heard about the Committee on Human Development at the University of Chicago (U of C). A fellow student told me he was admitted to this program for doctoral students and urged me to look into the program. I was intrigued by his description of a very liberal, intellectual, and philosophical perspective in such a renowned university. I was delighted when I received an invitation for an interview. I was interviewed by Rosalind Dymond Cartwright, PhD. She was a pioneer in the field of empathy and psychotherapy research. She was also one of the first women to make significant contributions to the science of sleep and dreams as well as the field of sleep medicine. She worked with Carl Rogers, PhD at the U of C where he hired her to oversee the many audio-taped psychotherapy sessions that he was conducting to test the effectiveness of client-centered therapy. In 1954, both Drs. Rogers and Cartwright edited the landmark book, *Psychotherapy and Personality Change*. After U of C, she held positions in sleep research at the University of Illinois College of Medicine and Rush University Medical Center.

My interview with Dr. Cartwright was one of the best I ever had. She was responsive, empathic, friendly, and kind. I felt like I was having a conversation with a friend. At no time was I anxious, felt I was interrogated or judged. Before the interview officially ended, Dr. Cartwright said that she would recommend to the admissions committee that I be accepted for doctoral studies in the Committee on Human Development.

The Committee on Human Development (HD) was part of the unique academic community at the U of C where, in addition to traditional academic departments of study, interdisciplinary committees were formed based upon the scholarship of preeminent faculty. HD was unique in that the full range of the social sciences was united in the study and research of human behavior. Bernice Neugarten, PhD and Robert Havinghurst, PhD were among the internationally known scholars in HD who provided their students with the perspective of integrating psychology, sociology, cultural anthropology, and biology from infancy to old age.

Besides courses required in these academic subjects, the doctoral examination required essays in all these subjects. There was another unique aspect to HD. Doctoral students who wished to become clinicians were able to have two majors; one in Human Development and one in Clinical Psychology taught by the Psychology Department. The experience in Clinical Psychology involved: one year of courses in clinical psychology, such as theories of personality development; psychological testing and comparative therapeutic methods; a one-year internship in an American Psychological Association approved program and a doctoral examination on a clinical issue. Dr. Rogers, in the psychology department and Heinz Kohut, MD, in the Department of Psychiatry taught the course, "Theories of Personality Development." Samuel Beck, PhD taught about the Rorschach Test and William Henry, PhD taught a course on the Thematic Apperception Test (TAT). This joint academic training in HD and Clinical Psychology provided a continued liberal education, expanding the vistas for understanding and researching human behavior from a democratic and humanistic philosophy.

It was at the U of C that I met the first of many of lifelong friends and colleagues. In 1962 during my doctoral studies, I got to know both Harold Kooden, PhD, and Alan Entin, PhD. We have remained close to this day and they have both contributed chapters to a book I edited with Harold.

University of Chicago: My First Training to Be a Psychotherapist

It was a natural development for me to take a clinical internship at the Counseling and Psychotherapy Research Center at the U of C. I was intellectually and emotionally connected to client-centered psychotherapy as I became attracted to Dr. Rogers' ideas and methods. I felt that phenomenology provided a philosophical underpinning of client-centered psychotherapy and the empathic focus of the clinical methodology was very appealing to me. But perhaps, the most appealing to me was that client-centered psychotherapy and the Counseling Center were developed and administered by psychologists, not the medical profession. Psychologists were in charge; they were not subservient to psychiatrists. One of my fellow students at U of C complained to me that his internship in a hospital was so demeaning as a psychology intern that he decided to go to medical school. At the Counseling Center, I was treated like a younger colleague who had the intellect, personality, and interpersonal functioning to become a client-centered (now called person-centered) psychotherapist. The PhD faculty of the Counseling Center, including Jack Butler, John Shlien, Fred Zimring, Eugene Gendlin, and Laura Rice, was a wonderful combination of academicians and astute clinicians who were kind, warm, and empathic individuals. They all became role models for my becoming a scholar/clinician. They still remain in my thinking and functioning from when I was a student. My intellectual, clinical, and interpersonal contact with them laid the groundwork for integrating Ferenczi's alternative perspectives for psychoanalysis.

I was Dr. Shlien's teaching assistant at The Counseling Center. He was very open, personal, and kind. There were times when he would invite me to have lunch with him at his house near the campus. What a wonderful experience – having a meal with a distinguished member of the university's faculty who was also a leader in the field of psychotherapy. Dr. Shlien was a clinician I greatly admired, both for his emotional openness and for his sense of humor. He made me feel I was able to become a capable psychotherapist.

Fred Zimring's office door was always open, and one day, I wandered in to get acquainted. To my great surprise and delight, we spoke for about an hour and began a wonderful friendship. In his office was a giant blackboard upon which he wrote his intellectual and theoretical thinking, a combination of formulas, diagrams, ideas, and private thoughts. He was one of the kindest, most lovable people I knew at the university. I chose him to be the chairman of my doctoral research. One night in the beginning of my research year, I had an idea for a research project. I stayed up all night, wrote my doctoral proposal, and called him the next morning to ask if I could come in at 9 a.m. and show him the proposal. We spent half an hour discussing before he approved it. That day, it was officially accepted by the doctoral committee.

Dr. Gendlin was Dr. Rogers' right hand man in the Department of Person-Centered Psychotherapy. I contacted Dr. Gendlin to supervise me, and he agreed. He was a first-rate intellectual, an empathic clinician, and a very likable human being. His astute observations in supervision left me with an indelible imprint about person-centered psychotherapeutic theory.

I did have the opportunity to have contact with Dr. Rogers in the late 1980s. I registered for his group experience at an American Psychological Association Conference in Philadelphia, PA. From this group experience and prior videos I had seen, Dr. Rogers impressed me as a remarkable psychotherapist and human being. He seemed devoid of defensiveness while expressing his ideas and methods in a clear and precise manner. He had no need to dominate or control; he was a very likable human being. I believe Dr. Rogers and Ferenczi had similar qualities.

My First Experience with Psychoanalysis

My first contact with a psychoanalyst occurred at the Counseling and Psychotherapy Research Center at the U of C. Erika Fromm, an academic clinical psychologist and trained psychoanalyst was a member of the Clinical Psychology section of the Psychology Department. Fromm was also a faculty member at the Counseling Center. I asked her and she agreed to be my tutor for my required doctoral clinical study paper. Working with her revealed her to be a warm, affectionate, and responsive person. We easily developed a friendship. Fromm was a trained hypnotist. As I was a dormitory head at one of the college residences, I asked if she would give the students a lecture and demonstration on hypnosis. She generously accepted the invitation. I assisted her in the demonstration as I was studying hypnosis under her supervision. My wife was pregnant with our son at that time, and we also decided to ask her to use hypnosis as a preparation for birth delivery. We were ecstatic about the excellent delivery process that Fromm's preparation provided for my wife and our son. The academic and the personal experience with Fromm contributed to a positive and emotionally comfortable feeling in having a professional and personal relationship with a psychoanalyst.

Choosing a Postdoctoral Institute for Psychotherapeutic Training

After finishing my academic studies at the U of C, my wife and I returned to New York City, my home town. Now, I needed to find a postdoctoral program in order to become a clinician. I was interested in studying at New York University's (NYU) Postdoctoral Program in Psychoanalysis and Psychotherapy as this program was within an academic setting. I felt it would have a more liberal and intellectual perspective. NYU also had adjunct faculty, such as Erich Fromm PhD, whom I admired. The Postgraduate Center for Mental Health was also of interest because Lewis Wolberg, MD, who was its founder and director, had an eclectic perspective. The Postgraduate Center, under Wolberg's directorship, was considered to have a reputation as a liberal analytic perspective. I felt that would allow for training from a variety of ideas and methods, thereby, orthodoxy.

I was interviewed as part of my application to NYU. I felt comfortable anticipating the interview with a NYU faculty member. I expected a liberal psychoanalytic interchange. Unfortunately, the interview was a disaster. The interviewer questioned me about my extracurricular activities. I naively volunteered that I was enjoying my new sports car, which I bought as a present for completing my doctoral studies. The interviewer interpreted that as the money spent on buying my car should have been spent on going into psychoanalysis. This criticism of my behavior was surprising and disconcerting. I felt the interviewer was an orthodox analyst and I did not fit his standard for a psychoanalyst. According to him, I should have been committed to analysis as an undergraduate if I wanted to be an analyst. As I expected, I was not admitted to NYU. This rejection was emotionally difficult because I felt NYU's program would be a meaningful stepping stone to integrating psychoanalysis with my prior education and experience.

My interview at the Postgraduate Center For Mental Health was completely different than my NYU experience. At the American Psychological Association Conference in the summer of 1964, I interviewed with Ted Reiss, PhD, the head of the research department of the Postgraduate Center, Asya Kadis, MA, head of its group department, and Manny Schwartz, PhD, dean of training.

The first interview, with Dr. Reiss, was an extremely positive and enjoyable experience. It was a friendly interchange between colleagues. Dr. Reiss was a warm, responsive, interesting, and likable individual. He clearly enjoyed our hour-long discussion and ended our meeting by saying that he would recommend me to the admissions committee.

I went from my interview at NYU, which made me feel I was not worthy of being a psychoanalytic trainee, to the Postgraduate Center experience where I was made to believe I was an exceptional analytic candidate. In addition, I was told I would receive one of two National Mental Health Postdoctoral Fellowships in Psychoanalysis and Psychotherapy. I felt I was going to feel comfortable in the psychoanalytic setting of the Postgraduate Center, as well as feel that I was a valued individual whose previous education and training was respected.

Postgraduate Center for Mental Health: a Difficult Beginning

I definitely felt like a stranger during the first year of my analytic training at the Postgraduate Center. I was the only candidate who was unfamiliar with the theory and method of psychoanalysis, especially the Freudian perspective. What is more, the other candidates wanted to become psychoanalysts from the time they entered college, in some instances, since they were in high school. It was clear these individuals believed becoming a psychoanalyst was the most prestigious, intellectual, and important profession to which they could aspire. Dr. Sigmund Freud was everyone's hero. During the training period, almost all male candidates grew full face beards in the style of the founder of psychoanalysis.

The start of my experience at the Postgraduate Center was very upsetting. The dean of training made a point of talking to me during the first day of my arriving at the Postgraduate Center. He said there was an issue about my attendance at the training program because I did not have my doctorate. I had not been able to present my doctoral dissertation at U of C in the spring or summer of 1964 because all of the doctoral committee members were not available to meet. The defense of my dissertation was scheduled for that September when I was starting at the Postgraduate Center. I had been concerned about beginning my analytic training without officially having my doctorate. I had called the Postgraduate Center and spoke to a member of the Postgraduate Training Committee who was also the head of the Psychology Department. I received permission to begin my training at the Postgraduate Center as I planned to take my doctoral oral examination that September.

The dean began our conversation by addressing me as Dr. Rachman. I thought I was being open and honest by telling him about my doctoral oral exams having not yet been completed. This dean had not been available when I spoke to the head of the Psychology Department. The dean then became furious with me and criticized me for coming to the Postdoctoral Center without my doctorate, claiming I threatened his postdoctoral program. I was shocked by his accusations. I told him I had called the head of the Psychology Department and received permission to attend before completing my oral exam. In addition, I had made preparations to take the exam in September which was also the same time the training program began. He acted as if he did not hear a word I said, and was not interested in my explanation. He continued his tirade and commanded me to make arrangements to take my doctoral examination. What is more, he assigned a faculty member to oversee that I fulfilled this requirement. I was furious at the dean's treatment. For about a week after this traumatic incident, I kept thinking about withdrawing from the program. I talked to my family and friends and decided I had not done anything wrong. I was not going to let this person defeat me.

Postgraduate Center for Mental Health: My Personal Psychoanalysis with Betty Feldman, MA

Finding a personal analyst also began on a negative note at the Postgraduate Center because of the same dean's authoritarian personality and manner. When I was called into the dean's office to discuss who was going to be my analyst, he told me he had three referrals he wanted me to contact. I told him that I had someone I wished to see. I had felt an emotional and positive interpersonal connection in the classroom to a particular faculty member. The dean responded that is not how things are done at the Postgraduate Center. Then he added that since I had been granted a National Institute for Mental Health Fellowship, the trainee rate for my psychoanalysis would not be reduced from $25 to $15 per session. I walked out of the dean's office depressed and angry. I could not choose the analyst I wanted. It was clear there was no confidentiality about my analysis and paying more for my analysis might prove difficult since I now had the responsibility of a wife and young son. The dean did not demonstrate any empathy or compassion for my needs; he was only interested in his rules and regulations.

I was determined never to let this dean force me out of this training program. There was no one during this early period I could turn to for advice. I did not think there was any faculty or supervisor who would stand up for me and my fellow trainees were preoccupied with trying to find analysts of their own. However, I was able to develop a plan for acquiring an analyst on my own.

During the beginning of my coursework, I took a class taught by Betty Feldman, MA, head of the Social Work Department. She impressed me as warm, kind, and thoughtful. I decided to contact her. In my meeting with her I asked if she would be my analyst. She clearly saw I was very upset about my struggle to find an analyst. After I told her about the difficulties I was having, I ended by saying that I am afraid the dean would not allow me to see her because he did not choose her. Her response felt like I had found an angel. She said that if she decides that we can work together to do analysis, no one can change that, not even the dean. I released a deep sigh and told Betty I was very grateful for her response to my struggle. This wonderfully helpful session with Betty, which solved my struggle to find a personal analyst, was an integral turning point for me in believing that I could become positively connected to the Postgraduate Center and its training program.

As I go over the memories of my experiences in analytic training, I believe my analysis with Betty was one of the most significant emotional, interpersonal, and intellectual highlights of my analytic training. As soon as we began our analysis, which involved four weekly individual analysis sessions and one group analytic session, I experienced Betty's genuine affection and empathy. Her concern, respect, and interest in me was clearly interwoven in our interaction in the analysis as well as in our other contacts. This analysis lasted the four years during the analytic training program. The end of the personal analysis was mutually agreed upon. My five sessions a week for four years seemed to help me uncover, analyze, and work through my fundamental neurotic issues: my mother's depression due to her thirty-two-year-old husband's death; the emotional absence of my father who died when I was nine years old; the essential role my grandmother played in providing the missing emotional interpersonal attachment I needed for my personality development; and my difficulties in interpersonal relationships. My view on what helped me the most in my analysis was having an analyst in Betty Feldman who believed in me. She believed that I was capable of forming an empathic relationship as a psychoanalyst. From the beginning of the analysis to its ending, she was openly friendly, affectionate, supportive, and affirmative. She was never silent and always ready to respond to me.

We could also have negative encounters. I felt safe, non-defensive, eager to hear what she thought about working on and through my emotional issues. If I did not agree with her interpretations, we could argue. She allowed me to contribute my thinking about the issue, and was open about how she felt about our differences. As I think about her empathy and being attuned to me, I would call our analysis a "two-person experience in a relationship." Betty's manner of conducting an analysis was similar to the person-centered psychotherapy of Dr. Rogers and the psychoanalysis of Ferenczi. When Betty passed, sadly after a long illness, I lost not only my former analyst but also one of the most important friends in my life, who contributed greatly to my emotional well-being.

I am also left with a very special memory of discussing with Betty a supervisory session I witnessed conducted by Lewis Wolberg, MD, the founder and distinguished director of the Postgraduate Center. She told me that Dr. Wolberg's analyst was Clara Thompson. Clara Thompson's analyst was Sándor Ferenczi. We both conjectured that Clara Thompson may have passed on Ferenczi's active, empathic, experimental approach in psychoanalysis to Wolberg. Betty and I went further with our conjectures. Our discussion resulted in our conclusion that I was a *fourth generation analysand of Sándor Ferenczi* in the following way:

1 Sándor Ferenczi analyzed Clara Thompson.
2 Clara Thompson analyzed Lewis Wolberg.
3 Lewis Wolberg analyzed Betty Feldman.
4 Betty Feldman analyzed Arnold Rachman.

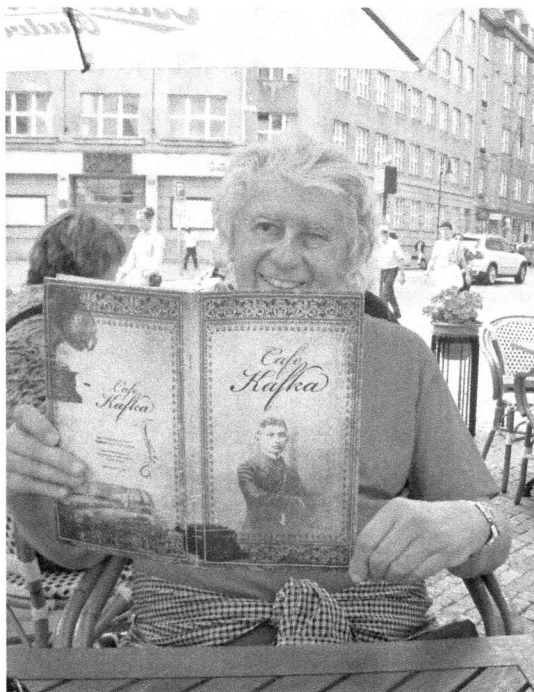

Figure 1 Arnold in Prague in 2012 celebrating his favorite author, Franz Kafka, by stopping at Café Kafka, located by Franz Kafka's birthplace on the Old Town Square.

Figure 2 Arnold posing by a photograph of Sándor Ferenczi in the Ferenczi House in Budapest, Hungary.

Figure 3 Arnold enjoying a day in Rio de Janeiro in 2004 on his way to presenting at the XIII International Forum of Psychoanalysis in Belo Horizonte, Brazil.

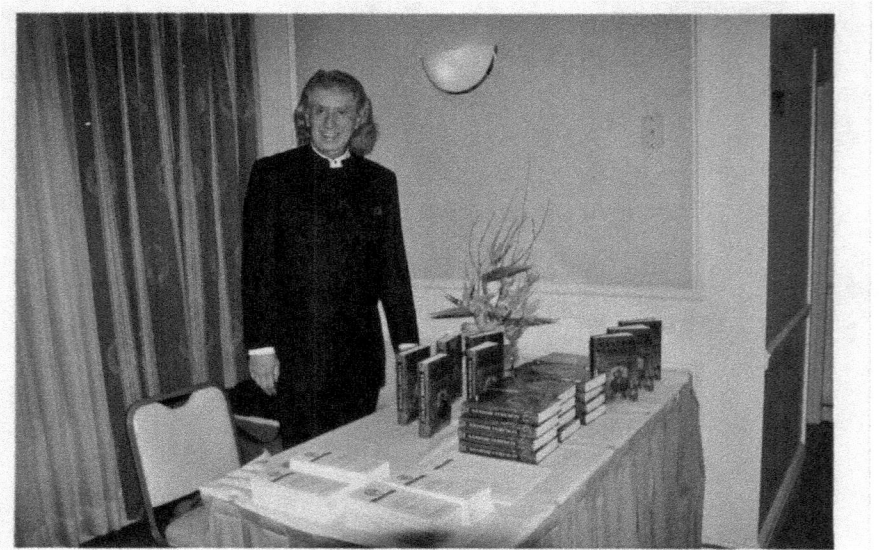

Figure 4 Arnold at a book signing for his first book, *Sándor Ferenczi: The Psychotherapist of Tenderness and Passion*.

Figure 5 Arnold enjoying dessert, his favorite course.

Figure 6 Arnold, well dressed, enjoying a family event.

2 Leota Brown Comes to Town

Fergal Brady

Leota Brown comes to town.

"During the time Severn was in analysis with Ferenczi, he produced his most controversial work. Severn was an integral part of this controversy. In fact, one could say. Severn instigated these controversies," (Rachman, 2018, p. 45).[1]

"You're damn right I did." Elizabeth, 2019.[1]

May 7th, 2019. Dundalk, Ireland

It's eight-thirty in the morning. Back to work at the day job after a holiday weekend. No holiday here, too busy with preparations for our conference this coming weekend. The Budapest School of Psychoanalysis. From Ferenczi, the Balints and Beyond will be staged in Dublin starting Friday.

I have just closed down my email, making final contacts and plans with colleagues coming from opposite ends of Ireland, from Budapest and New York.

Marcus, traveling on Friday from Cork to talk to us about Freud and the Seduction Theory. Christine coming from Belfast, in the North to fill us in on the work of the Balints and demonstrate a Balint Group. There's Judit coming from Budapest to update us on contemporary lines of Ferenczian thought. And Arnold. Arnold is traveling from New York with his wife, Nancy. I'm meeting them at Dublin Airport on Thursday morning our time. We'll find out Saturday who else might be traveling with him. A stowaway if you like.

I nearly met her a year ago. She proves illusive. Or maybe she doesn't. Maybe we were the illusive ones. Failing to see her.

Because with three days to go until a conference I have been organizing since last fall I am still not sure if the guest of honor will make an appearance. When I write that and when I think about it, this is my principal motivation for promoting the conference in the first place. I want to see if she comes. In fact, I am trying to make the conditions right for her to appear so we can let her know that we can see her and hear her. And maybe, like Florence last year, nobody will fully notice her there.

DOI: 10.4324/9781003391081-2

I'll try to explain. Her spirit made an appearance and, frankly, caused a bit of trouble.

So, we go back in time, in order to go forward, in the best traditions of psychoanalysis.

May 6th, 2018. Convitto del Calza, Firenze

Elizabeth is granted three wishes.

It is the 13th International Sándor Ferenczi Conference and Arnold begins his talk "Elizabeth Severn as a Person, Clinician, and Collaborator of Sándor Ferenczi." He describes how he came into possession of Elizabeth Severn's papers. Her daughter, Margaret, had died, leaving an executor in possession of Elizabeth's papers.

A colleague had told the executor of Arnold's interest in Elizabeth and put them in touch. Arnold couldn't believe his luck. He had been unaware of the voluminous collection of her papers. Indeed, nobody in the analytical community knew of them. This, for an author, analyst, and historical researcher of Arnold's renown is the equivalent of sitting in disbelief, clutching a winning lottery ticket.

There would be more welcome surprises. There was an interview that Elizabeth had given to Kurt Eissler, the keeper of the keys, the founder and director of the Freud Archives. That interview, recorded on December 20, 1952 was previously unknown to Ferenczi scholars.

Arnold continues his talk, we're still in Florence, and the year is still 2018. We didn't know this yet, but as Arnold spoke, something was stirring in the underworld.

Arnold went on to outline how Elizabeth had changed her name to Elizabeth Severn, replacing her previous identity as Leota Loretta Brown, the exiled and abused girl of her childhood. This was Elizabeth's first wish. To leave Leota behind, let her rest in the past. She wished to be Leota no more and to forge her new identity as Elizabeth. Her first wish is outlined. One rub of the lamp.

She worked for a time, Arnold explained, as an encyclopedia sales person, discovering in the process a latent talent. Elizabeth could draw people out. Traces of Leota, seeking out, drawing out the other, were seeping through to her new identity from her past.

Elizabeth's talent for connecting with something within and even soothing something in the other surfaced again at the hair salon. She perhaps "impersonated" a massage therapist, reassuring an angry client who had been let down. Elizabeth carried out this metamorphosis effortlessly as she had been doing all her life. She was satisfied for the moment, content to see how long she could occupy the identity of "therapist" before maybe it began to come unstuck, as it often did.

Pretty soon she conjured up the role of metaphysician, combining her newfound talents into a person she now began to grow into.

She had repeatedly struggled to make any of these roles and identities stick for any length of time. Their fickle foundations in Milwaukee, Wisconsin repeatedly intruded and caused them to crumble. She sought professional help, moving through two analysts before finding herself under the care of Otto Rank who she found "completely wrapped up in the one idea of the birth trauma, and incapable of thinking of anything else" (Rachman, 2018, p. 110). Finding her analysis with Rank unsatisfactory she finished and looked farther afield, Rank recommending Ferenczi.

Elizabeth wished to become secure in her new identity. This was her second wish and, in outlining it to his audience, Arnold had inadvertently given a second rub of the lamp in which Leota's spirit rested, somewhat uneasily.

At this too, there were the first stirrings of unease in the room. I felt it like a gust of dry wind. Having her story told was what she wanted, but it made her restless, eager to let out the full affect of it all. The first traces of a gap in the space–time continuum were beginning to emerge. These manifested in the room with some minor technical glitches with the projector, images of Elizabeth, and with time. It began to become expressed in an agitated manner about Arnold's presentation running out of time. In the real world, in 2018, the presentation of her case was mirroring the way it always went, poorly and with misunderstandings. Really, it was the spirit of Elizabeth, restless, still, after all these years, wishing to find an ear that was attuned to her, could hear her, and could set Leota free. And not for the first time, no matter how much she raged she could find no one to hear.

Elizabeth's third wish was seeking expression. Although nobody in the room seemed to be conscious of what was happening, Arnold continued, caressing the lamp, drawing on Elizabeth's excited and increasingly restless spirit.

She had found her way to Sándor at this point in the story and had become frustrated with him. She could see the potential in him. She knew that Sándor could be the one to set her free, to help fulfil her third wish.

But, unknown to him at the time, he was standing in her way, blocking her path.

"Sándor," she protested, "*you* are getting in *my* way, it's not *me*, it's *you*."

Eventually, sincere and tender as he was, he conceded that she was right. He stood aside and Elizabeth came to life. But at this exact point in the tale, the vibrations in the room became stronger and Arnold, in telling her story and building the narrative, had rubbed the lamp a third time and POOFF!

Elizabeth appeared in the room.

She looked around. No one could see her. She saw the frail ghost of Sigmund Freud sitting uncomfortably to the side, his face a little reddened from being challenged, his doctrine contradicted.

She fixed him with a glare, her eyes narrowed.

"Evil Genius eh? FUCK YOU."

All hell broke out in the room but nobody seemed fully conscious as to why. Arnold had evoked the spirit of Elizabeth and she demanded her third wish. Elizabeth's wish to become alive, expressed to and through Sándor opened a portal to the past to the traumatized Leota who had a story to tell that nobody had fully succeeded in listening to, to date. It was always too difficult for the listener to bear. What had happened to Leota one hundred and thirty years before was still too threatening for an audience to hear. She had been asked to bear this alone all these years and she needed someone to be able to travel back to it with her and to be able to bear it with her. Was that too much to ask? It ended badly, like it always did. Arnold's presentation had to be cut short, in the real world he simply ran out of time. But it meant that, again, Leota did not get heard.

May 7th, 2019. Dundalk, Ireland

So, back to 2019 and the Dublin conference. I get an email from Judit. I had written about how excited I was and how much I was looking forward to showing people the fabulous venue for our conference. There were lots of organizational bits and pieces to be sorted. Judit finished her email saying that the spirit of Ferenczi would see me through. I felt it. Something is rising and it could be very special.

May 9th, 2019. Dublin, Ireland

Thursday morning, I am on the road early to meet the Rachmans at the airport. We have a great day together, them acclimatizing to Ireland (it's cool for the time of year) and recovering from their transatlantic flight and time lag. We enjoy a meal together and they turn in for the night early.

I take a walk out the front of the hotel around the library and Lexicon venue where the conference will be held. Eight-thirty at night, early May, it's a bright, cool evening. I have a walk along the seafront and it comes to me. She is here. And suddenly I am overcome with emotion. This immediately followed with a fear that I will become emotional at the conference, in my address even. Settle down I tell myself, it's going to be great. But she's here all right, I can feel her.

I'm trying to tune in to her. What is Elizabeth to her? She became Elizabeth. Elizabeth saved her, I guess. Gave her a new identity, a new start, many new starts in fact. Leota kept morphing and changing and searching, searching. This was no butterfly emerging analogy here, this was serious. And the ghosts that set the young Leota on her journey still haunted the corridors of her mind. She still needed to keep running, keep changing, hold onto whatever she could of a facsimile identity. Because she still had not succeeded in exorcising those ghosts.

That doctor tried. The Doctor of tenderness and passion Arnold called him. He was that all right. But I taught him that. Nobody ever says that. Arnold does in ways, I guess. Leota emerges screaming, raging, hating. Trying to make herself heard. Why can nobody tune in to her frequency?

She got mad with the tender Doctor on a few occasions. She could see that he was the one man who could unlock the deepest parts of it. But sometimes he was so frustrating and so blocked up himself that I needed to change places with him to give him the final whoosh I needed to have Leota heard.

And then it all died down for decades. Until, as the story goes, Arnold got a phone call and someone told him that they had Elizabeth's papers. The grown-up Elizabeth had written it all down. Her story and Leota's.

Ferenczi, the kind Doctor of Budapest had written it too. In a secret diary. He knew he would get in trouble if it all came out. If he told what we did and what I said and what he said. We'd all get in awful trouble. We all know that. Every boy and girl who has been touched knows that, their dirty secret underworld which they don't want told. The kind Doctor did a good enough job of that. Because he wanted to listen and he wanted to understand and, god love him, he wanted to help. He had a kind smile. Patient. Even when you are being horrible to him. Because he is so slow. My god. This is exhausting.

I'm not sure who is possessed here. Or who is possessed with what. I just know there's a little girl who wants to tell what happened. And she wants someone to listen and know that it's the truth and not feel sorry or not sympathize but just acknowledge it and nod agreement and communicate acceptance and most important of all not to judge. You can see it in some of them. It makes them uncomfortable and they look down and they want it shut down, that makes me mad. Just hear it. I'm not asking anything of you. Just hear it. And respect me.

May 11th 2019, Dún Laoghaire, Ireland

The day finally arrives. A bright, cool sunny morning dawns and delegates begin to gather at the venue at the seafront in the Harbour at Dún Laoghaire. Every one arrives, a good contingent from Belfast, Judit Mészáros from Budapest, and Arnold and his wife, Nancy from New York.

Arnold, as I have described it, is the second or third most important guest. In front of him in the roll of honor are the twin psyches of Elizabeth and Leota Loretta Brown. I have spent the last few nights re-reading key chapters of Arnold's book about Elizabeth, Elizabeth Severn, the "Evil Genius of Psychoanalysis." I have some thoughts. In particular, I have some thoughts about where Leota resides.

As I review my writing from the night before, I wonder if anybody will be able to make any sense of it. I understand Bion this morning, a psychoanalytic grandson of Sándor Ferenczi, because of the merging of Leota Loretta, Elizabeth, and Margaret Severn with my psyche. I was getting mad on Thursday night at psychoanalysis for not being able to hear her/me.

Arnold has recovered well from his trans-Atlantic flight and arrives at the 21st-century library building in fine fettle. He warmly greets delegates and settles himself in for what will be a long day of presentations. We have music playing in the theater as folk arrive. Gershwin, "Rhapsody in Blue," to make a

New Yorker feel at home. With five minutes to go to the beginning of the day's events the Indiana Jones theme plays loudly in the Hall. Psychoanalysis, the archaeology of the mind. Scratching with our metaphorical trowel at the surface levels. Uncovering the dirt, moving backwards through time to uncover artifacts which will give us clues to past events. These musical pieces picked by design to set the scene for what is hoped will be a great day's presentations during which we can bring the spirit of the Budapest School to life. The V.I.P. guest then, Leota Loretta can make her appearance.

Leota Loretta the first only gets a bit part in the theater of the whole thing. She is further represented by Elizabeth, her older, adult self. But what has become clear is that she also lived, restlessly, in Margaret, her daughter. If you know how to tune into Leota's frequency you will have no trouble working out why Margaret burned her correspondence with her mother. Its no mystery, although scholars represent it as one. In moments, the unbearable presence of Leota takes the controls in Margaret's psyche and she rages to be heard.

Ferenczi brought to life a girl who would have been forgotten if her adult self had not been referred to him by Rank. That adult self turned up at Ferenczi's Budapest office and, struggling to bear and contain the traumatized Leota, demanded to be seen and to be properly heard.

Elizabeth had already done some amazing work in various incarnations of various careers on various towns restlessly trying to find some peace for Leota.

These doctors, mostly men, had their frankly useless interpretative technique. Silent listening followed by self-gratifying intellectual summaries based on a marriage to concepts thought up by some other man in some other town who is not present to experience how Leota FEELS.

Sándor tried; he too was wed to the technique from Vienna. She could sense his resistance, his inner woman hatred. She knew from her own work and experimentation that in the trance state she had discovered she could go to places within herself where the torment lay. And she knew that being able to experience it in the kindly presence of an attuned other can settle something of the bubbling, fermenting torment of trying to lay to rest what she saw and what was done to her. What was done to her little body. Many of the people who hear this cannot bear it. Cannot bear how it feels. Cannot bear how it makes them feel. Because you can't think your way out of this one, you have to feel it. And if you are going to help Leota you have to be able to bear how it feels, not how it felt, how it still feels to be her.

Elizabeth endured a whole year of Sándor's resistances while she fought with him about her care. Eventually she had to get mad with him. He couldn't hear her because of his own prejudices and fixed sets of beliefs about things. She persisted with him because he was kind, because she knew that he felt hurt at times and dissatisfied at not being able to settle her. In his discomfort at the lack of progress of her care she saw the possibilities if she could align his psyche with her's and create a portal back to Loreta which could free her of this unbearable torment. She could communicate with him extra sensorily.

He had the grace, Sándor, eventually to admit that she was right. He had enough of the feminine within him to set aside the master's influence within him, to be able to give her the floor and direct the course of her own analysis. That Master, Freud, in Vienna, didn't like Elizabeth very much. Felt threatened by her. She wasn't going to let that get in her way of Leota's coming out.

There was a debutant's ball being prepared for the nascent Leota's settled self and no Doctor man miles away in Vienna was going to be allowed to prevent it happening.

After the failure to be heard in Florence, the organizers of this Dublin event had liaised with Arnold and made available to him whatever time he needed to set Leota free. The first draft of the conference program had allocated two full hours to the Evil Genius of Psychoanalysis. In later re-drafts as the day got nearer, Arnold had said he could deliver his presentation in sixty to ninety minutes. So, it was decided. Eleven-thirty to one in the afternoon was set aside for Arnold to work his magic and set Leota free. I had done all I could setting the scene, gathering a crowd of people to witness and to hear, all we needed now was for the story to be told and the conditions would be right for her to be felt.

The conduit is the key. The gap in space–time back to the girl can only be opened by someone who feels it. Someone who feels it, not a little, but a lot. There had to be a feeling of outrage to out the rage, so to speak. Arnold describes Elizabeth's hairdresser role, her massage therapy incarnation, the beginnings of her therapist incarnation. A sort of time travel worthy of the various lives and incarnations of Doctor Who. And, of course, as I had hoped it would, the restlessness begins to stir in the audience, we are so caught up in our trainings and the rules about what you are allowed to say. And what knowledge you have to gain before you are allowed into the privileged set who are allowed to dispense the interpretive solutions to the problems patients bring that many can't bear to admit Elizabeth, this self-proclaimed, psychotherapist interloper. Was she a doctor someone asked? How, another wondered, did she find time to study to be a therapist while working as an encyclopedia sales person. That's the one, I think, which gets the whole uneasy reaction to her started. How dare she throw out that old line about people opening up to her as she calls at their door selling books. You have to have years of specialized training to be able to get people to open up to you. You could do untold damage otherwise, we have training standards, these things are regulated now, even by governments, to protect the public from charlatans. This lady gets right under the skin of the whole profession by stomping right in to the middle of the conference and demanding to be let in and given a voice.

Leota, set free, is a challenge to the whole practice of psychoanalysis.

That's what Arnold does. Within his admirable scholarly work there burns the rage at the injustice that was done to Ferenczi, "it still makes me crazy, the more I think about it" he tells us in his presentation. I sat beside him when he made his presentation. I loved it. His paper was handwritten and dated April 30, 2019. Less than two weeks old.

He moves on to talk about Uma Thurman and her descriptions in a recent interview of her sexual trauma at the hands of movie-maker men. The "Confusion of Tongues" paper, handwritten, not yet typed, absolutely contemporary. A woman, an actor, who was still a girl when the movie-makers got her. She eloquently voiced what it was like. She had a framework, a roadmap to describe what had happened to her. There is a language now to be able to map the key points along the road of an abusive relationship. Arnold delivers it with an amount of indignant outrage. Appropriate outrage. Because you can't set the trauma free unless you can be outraged in the present about what happened in the past. And in that, it only works if you feel enough affinity, respect, outrage at what was done and what the girl endured and how her voice was silenced in it. How the power overwhelmed her young psyche to the point where she becomes controlled by the man who exercises the control to the end in service of his own sexual gratification.

Leota helped frame the language through which Uma Thurman could be heard. Leota became Elizabeth, a stronger, more determined version of herself. She found this doctor who wanted to be able to listen. You can't accept the title "The analyst of last resort" or "The analyst of difficult cases" if you turn people away saying "you can't be helped."

In the end, it is actually very simple. But you have to allow your Self to be enlisted in it. Arnold does that. He puts himself in the firing line. He feels it. Right now. At night, after the conference, we retire to a local Italian place for a bit to eat and a get-together to unwind.

Arnold tells me about his experience. A draft of a paper about Elizabeth, first accepted, then rejected for publication. It is too controversial. Arnold is not included in the cast of characters, analysts, interviewed for the Hungarian television documentary about Ferenczi. He should have been included, he insists, asking Judit, playfully, but earnestly, why he was overlooked.

He kind of rages for a moment. That's how you set Leota free. You have to get a little bit crazy. I want to give him a hug. I want to say it's okay Arnold; you are doing it right. You have done it right. You have shown me how it is done. Not only in your admirable scholarly work; but also, on your wonderful, lovely self, getting mad.

May 12th, 2019. Dún Laoghaire, Ireland

It is six o'clock in the morning and I'm sitting in my hotel room writing. I have been up since half four. I placed my most recent copy of Arnold's book *The Evil Genius* on the table beside me as I write. My unconscious guided me to put it there because on the table opposite there's a small pile of other books which I left there.

I open the book and read the inscription.

May 10, 2019.
  Dear Fergal,
  Keep Ferenczi alive in your work and life.
  Warmly,
  A.

I will Arnold, I will. Mind yourself.

Note

1 One of these quotes is "reconstructed."

Reference

Rachman, A. *Elizabeth Severn. The "Evil Genius" of Psychoanalysis*. London and New York, Routledge, 2018.

3 Tribute

Jill Choder-Goldman

I have had the pleasure of knowing Dr. Arnold Rachman since 2003 when I was a psychoanalytic candidate in training at The National Institute for the Psychotherapies. I'm thrilled to say that we have been in each other's lives since then and I would like to share with you how our relationship began because that speaks volumes as to why we are still in each other's lives.

I met Dr. Arnold Rachman when I was in my third year of analytic training and was assigned a three times a week patient, with a woman in her forties who was described as bipolar, had Borderline Personality Disorder, and was an extremely difficult patient to work with overall. And if that wasn't sufficient to scare me off, her psychiatrist told me that psychoanalytic exploration would never work with a patient like this. As a student, I was scared and intimidated and feared that this was a recipe for disaster.

I interviewed Dr. Rachman to be my supervisor because he had a reputation for being a psychoanalyst who worked with "extremely difficult patients" and this person fell into that category. When we finished our meeting, I asked him "do you think you and I will be a good match for this patient?" He took a beat, looked me straight in the eyes and said, "I don't know, we'll have to see."

I left his office wondering if he liked me and if this relationship could work, but I knew that he was really smart and good with those kinds of patients. So, with great trepidation, I decided to go for it.

We began our work the next week and I realized that my feelings of uncertainty and fear couldn't have been further from reality and the truth.

Arnold and I worked for the next year with this very difficult and challenging patient, but I can't imagine any other supervisor who would've helped me work so deeply to understand this patient's fits and who would've stood by me when those fits were directed at me.

I can remember one day that the patient didn't show up. She called to say she wasn't coming in and in fact she wasn't sure if she even wanted to continue with me. She was in a manic rage and I could hear that she was literally throwing her dishes against the wall while she hurled insult after insult at me and then hung up.

My countertransference was through the roof. At that moment I hated her, was frightened of her and did not want to see or work with her ever again.

DOI: 10.4324/9781003391081-3

I panicked as she was my control case and I needed her to be in treatment for one year. I called Arnold in desperation and after listening to what happened, he calmly said: "Call her now and stay on the phone with her no matter what state she's in. With empathic resonance, tell her that you understand how angry she is but that she needed to come in tomorrow for our session so we could talk about it and understand why she was so enraged at me."

I told Arnold my strong countertransferential feelings and that I felt hopeless about the treatment. His response, which I have never forgotten all these years was, "if we lose hope in our patients, they will as well and there's no treatment. We must always hold the hope for them." He was absolutely right in insisting I call her back and tell her that I would see her as planned the next morning. What I was saying to her was that I can tolerate your anger, and I will not punish you or leave you because of it, like your mother did. The treatment changed after that episode. It got deeper and more authentic.

That would've never happened if Arnold Rachman was not my supervisor.

That was 2004 and we have been in each other's lives since then. Working together as colleagues, as my supervisor, as a teacher, and sometimes even as a personal confidant. Arnold is always there and available.

Dr. Rachman is a scholar who has written fourteen books on everything from incest trauma, tenderness and passion, the psychotherapy of difficult cases, Elizabeth Severn, and copious works on Sándor Ferenczi. However, that is just one special part of Arnold.

As a participant in my life he has not only been an educator, and a supervisor but an amazing human being and friend.

His empathy, not only for his patients but his students as well, goes above and beyond. But that's not to say that Dr. Rachman is not challenging and 100 percent honest with those he works with. He won't hesitate to challenge you, tell you he doesn't agree with you, and be willing to engage in deep conversation about the differences in how you might see things.

Knowing Dr. Arnold Rachman for over fifteen years has been a tremendous addition in both my professional and personal life.

I cannot say enough about a man who has touched so many in so many ways and I am honored to be one of those people.

4 Following in Sándor Ferenczi's Footsteps

A Festschrift in Honor of Arnold William Rachman, PhD: a Writer's Writer: the Psychoanalyst Arnold W. Rachman

Ann D'Ercole

"Everybody writes their first book with a certain innocence, of vision. 'The writer's writer' …. writes every book that way."

(Jhumpi Lahiri, 2011)

What a wonderful moment of celebration for this journal to address the intellectual contributions of Arnold William Rachman, a preeminent psycho-historian, outstanding clinician, and a scholar. His writings are infused with his thoughtfulness, clarity, and foresight. His writing is always fresh and refreshing as he delivers a new understanding of psychoanalysis and its methods to historians and clinicians. His scholarly work includes more than twenty-four published essays and books.

My acquaintance with Dr. Rachman is relatively recent. On June 26, 2018, I wrote to Dr. Rachman at the suggestion of my colleague at the New York University Postdoctoral Program in Psychotherapy and Psychoanalysis, the late Lewis Aron. Lew was aware of my developing research project, a biography of the American psychiatrist and psychoanalyst, Clara Mabel Thompson. He suggested that, since Thompson had been Ferenczi's analysand and student, I try contacting Arnold Rachman, an expert on Sándor Ferenczi's work.

It turns out Lew's suggestion was a gift. Arnold immediately responded to my email. In his reply, he shared some of his ideas suggesting whom to contact next, which libraries to search, and others who might be approached for information. His generosity was not limited to this encounter. When I expressed my sincere appreciation, he kindly asked, "Would you like to meet to talk about the project?" My response was an immediate, "yes."

Writing can be a lonely enterprise, having only your thoughts and your relationship with the material to keep you company. In working with Arnold, I found someone with whom to share both my ideas and my connection with the material. He is an inspiring, "writer's writer."

Our first meeting lasted for two hours. Our conversation moved easily between our mutual writing projects and our many overlapping views about our shared profession and experiences. We had in common a fondness for one of my former analysts, Dr. Esther Menaker. We shared some of our memories of her as we talked about Clara Thompson and Ferenczi. Our meetings

DOI: 10.4324/9781003391081-4

continued over the next months as Arnold generously became my companion on my research journey into the life and work of Clara Thompson. He, like his self-claimed mentor, Ferenczi, created a particular emotional atmosphere where ideas flourished. I remember the day I discovered a stash of Thompson's letters in an archival library and communicated my discovery to Arnold. His excitement matched my elation. We discussed the meaning of an unpublished letter from Clara Thompson to Erich Fromm regarding Ferenczi's famous paper, "The Confusion of Tongues between Adults and the Child" (1932) and its place in the history of psychoanalysis. As we deliberated on the meaning of Thompson's November 5, 1957 letter to Erich Fromm (held in the Erich Fromm Archive, Tubingen), Arnold's depth of psychoanalytic history was quickly revealed. In the letter, Thompson confirms that Ferenczi was constantly afraid of losing Freud's approval and struggled to present his own ideas.

Rachman (1988) has written extensively about Freud and Ferenczi's relationship, a twenty-five-year friendship and collaboration that ultimately floundered because Ferenczi dared to step outside Freud's official clinical techniques and theories. That disruption began around the concept of empathy. At first, Ferenczi received Freud's approval for developing a new concept since Freud saw Ferenczi's use of empathy as an extension of his own use of tact (Rachman, p. 217). Freud had advised that tact was important in presenting an interpretation to a patient. Ferenczi, however, urged analysts to "follow the rule of empathy" when working with more difficult patients. An excellent discussion of that development is found in Rachman's 1988 essay, "The Rule of Empathy: Sándor Ferenczi's Pioneering Contributions to the Empathic Method in Psychoanalysis." In that essay, he quotes Clara Thompson on Ferenczi extensively, something few authors have done. Thompson's description of Ferenczi in many ways complements the interpersonal characteristics of Arnold Rachman:

> Possessed of a genuine sympathy for all human suffering, he approached each new day with an enthusiastic belief in his ability to help and in the worthwhileness of a patient. His efforts were tireless and his patience inexhaustible. He was never willing to admit that some mental diseases were incurable, but always said, "Perhaps it is simply that we have not yet discovered the right method." He completely lacked the pompous, important air and authoritative manner so common to many physicians. He won the confidence of his patients by making them feel that they have found a friend who would use all of his intelligence to help them. His simplicity encouraged them to lay aside their pretenses.
>
> (Thompson, 1964, p. 66)

Thompson also thought that Ferenczi wanted Freud to believe that he was only slightly modifying his theory (Thompson interview, 1952). But that was not true. Freud could not tolerate his disciple establishing himself and his ideas separately and Ferenczi was too fond of his mentor to tolerate his possible rejection. Their relationship broke down.

A debt is owed to Arnold Rachman for providing a complete picture of how Ferenczi's insights and improvements to psychoanalysis evolved in his impressive book *Sándor Ferenczi: The Psychotherapist of Tenderness and Passion* (Rachman, 1997).

I think the story of Rachman's inquiry into Ferenczi's use of the German term *Nachgiebigkeit* exemplifies his character. Ferenczi used the term *Nachgiebigkeit* to designate his new complementary rule to the principle of psychoanalytic absence. The word was translated into English as "indulgence" but Arnold wisely recognized that translation carried a negative connotation. After consulting with German-speaking colleagues in the United States and Europe, he suggested that a more modern translation of the concept was in fact, "flexibility." His diligent scholarship delivered a more accurate understanding of Ferenczi's clinical approach – one that captured the notion of a yielding and a willingness to give – offering a more positive, humanistic understanding. I trust that Elizabeth Severn, Izette de Forest, and Clara Thompson, three of Ferenczi's patients, would agree. Each of these analysands spoke to Ferenczi's generosity, tenderness, and love, characteristics consistent with a willingness to give and a sense of yielding.

Rachman's colleague André E. Haynal suggests that Rachman's book, *The Psychotherapist of Tenderness and Passion*, published in 1997, is "necessary reading for anyone who wants to be up to date on the understanding of … psychoanalytic thinking and especially psychoanalytic practice." *The Psychotherapist of Tenderness and Passion* not only delivers the history of a then relatively unknown Ferenczi to the psychoanalytic world but it also introduces the world to the clinical practice of working with traumatized and abused patients, thus bringing contemporary analysts a new understanding of the psychoanalytic method as developed by Ferenczi.

Fortunately Rachman brought our attention to Elizabeth Severn, Ferenczi's difficult patient and the person who helped him develop his new techniques (Rachman, 2018). The Ferenczi and Severn collaboration, he argues, resulted in a theory of trauma. *Elizabeth Severn: The "Evil Genius" of Psychoanalysis*, his book published in 2018, provides a view of psychoanalysis from the other side of the couch. It also situates her case as an iconic case like that of Freud's Dora and Anna O.

As a feminist scholar I am gratified that he has rescued Elizabeth Severn, an important woman in psychoanalytic history, from obscurity through his discovery of her papers. When Rachman was offered the purchase of the papers of Elizabeth Severn he said it was, "a dream come true" (Rachman, 2018, p. 32). Arnold purchased the Severn papers and deposited them in the Library of Congress for future scholars. That gesture reveals so much about the intellectual giant that I have come to know, his overall generosity and commitment to scholarship.

Rachman justly observed how "Psychoanalysis has had a love–hate relationship with the seduction theory and the treatment of the incest trauma," (Rachman and Klett, 2015, p. 17) and his work on the subject has greatly advanced our knowledge about the treatment of incest and trauma (Rachman and Klett, 2015). He continues to advocate for increased training in the area of treating patients who suffer from sexual trauma.

Dr. Rachman has many more intellectual contributions to make to our field. He is at work on a book on the Wolf-man that will turn the myth of Oedipus within psychoanalysis around. It will situate it where it rightly belongs, as a possible side note rather than a leitmotif.

The New Yorker (2011) ran a panel on the writer's writer's writer where each author, writers of fiction, offered up their own writer's writers, explaining their choices and reading from favorite stories. They argued that their choices most likely provide an insight into their own writing choices. I would agree. For anyone interested in psychoanalytic writing, reading Arnold Rachman's eye-opening psychoanalytic books and essays is indispensable to the process.

References

Rachman, A. The rule of empathy: Sándor Ferenczi's pioneering contributions to the empathic method in psychoanalysis, *Journal of American Academy of Psychoanalysis,* 16(1): 1–27, 1988 (p. 11).

Rachman, A. *Sándor Ferenczi: The Psychotherapist of Tenderness and Passion.* Northvale, NJ: Jason Aronson, 1997.

Rachman, A. *Elizabeth Severn: The "Evil Genius" of Psychoanalysis.* New York: Routledge, 2018.

Rachman, A. and Klett, S. *Analysis of the Incest Trauma: Retrieval, Recovery, Renewal.* London: Karnac, 2015.

5 A Fifty-Year Tribute to Arnold Rachman

Mark Feldman

I first met Dr. Rachman when I was seven years old. My mother and stepfather sent me to see him in order to help me consider an issue that we had in our family. My stepfather wanted to adopt me legally. My mom and stepfather, being fairly progressive for 1969, suggested that I see a therapist to discuss the possibility. And that's how we met. Now, fifty years later (as I write this), I am still his patient. I haven't been under his counsel for all of this time. We've taken breaks and we even lost touch for a while. But when I needed help, he was always the first person I thought of. And he was always there to help me.

Saying that Dr. Rachman has helped me would be a big understatement. But, yes, he has certainly helped me a great deal. He's seen me through two marriages and two divorces, a ten-year courtship with a woman who is now my wife and the mother of my daughter, and much more. I am very happily married. And very happy as a father. But neither of those relationships, in my opinion, would have been possible without Arnold's counsel. However, he's never told me what to do, although I've tried my hardest to get him to do so.

Dr. Rachman has been my rock, my advisor, my most trusted confidant. He has been an emotional archaeologist who pushed me to uncover the reasons for my sometimes less than optimal decisions (a big understatement!).

Amazingly, over time, it pretty much all got figured out. But that would not have happened without the therapy we did together. I had buried some important family issues and Dr. Rachman helped me uncover them. Those revelations made it clear that my repetitive behaviors (which often led to big problems) were linked to buried issues. I have no training in psychology, but I'll give you my simple layman version of what we discovered and how it changed my life.

My parents were divorced when I was 3 or 4. My mother left my biological father (and took me away with her) because, as she told me, he was cheating on her. I believe her. They were both in their twenties at the time, and after their split, my father was distant from me. He was constantly disappointing me in many ways. He'd consistently be late in picking me up for my weekend visits with him. He didn't talk much, and I don't recall much warmth from him. He was a "tough guy." Luckily, my stepfather was (and is) a gem. He was warm, encouraging, and doted on me. He was (and still is) a real father to me,

DOI: 10.4324/9781003391081-5

and it's not surprising that the decision arrived at when I was seven was to allow the adoption to take place.

Interestingly, but perhaps not surprising, was the fact that my genetic father did not fight the adoption at all. Later, I discovered that there was money involved. My father owed child support money, and him allowing the adoption granted him that the debt would be forgiven. So, he traded me for money. And now, as a father myself, the above is so much more shocking and unimaginable to me. Never, ever, in a million years, would I "give away" my daughter in that type of situation (were I to be unlucky enough to face such a choice).

Being rejected by one's father has severe consequences. But with Dr. Rachman's help, I began to understand what I had been up against. I realized that was one of the keys to my difficulties. Facing my biological father when I was in my thirties was an important event that Dr. Rachman and I planned out. Those meetings with my father and my attempt to discuss his relationship with my mother (I say "attempt" because he wasn't willing to discuss much) helped me greatly. I was able to confirm what I hypothesized about him. And then I was able to confront him.

I'm far from perfect, but I've been able to function at a much higher level with the knowledge I have about my past and my ability to face it. And I would not have been able to do these things and achieve this peace and understanding were it not for Dr. Arnold Rachman. I honor him and will always be thankful for his patience, wisdom, and counsel. He's a wonderfully intelligent, warm, and evolved man. I'm forever grateful to him and the kindness and guidance he has given me.

6   A Love Letter from a Former Client

Alan Fishman

It is a great pleasure to reflect on my experience as a client of Dr. Arnold Rachman.

Most of my experience was related to participation in his "group" therapy sessions in New York City over a period of about ten years. These group sessions involved a shifting number of participants with generally about seven to eight people present. My experiences with Arnold included two marathon sessions one of which lasted 24 hours.

I had been to another therapist before seeing Arnold and had been disappointed in that experience. I remember vividly my first appointment with Arnold. I explained in some detail the dramatic reasons for my situation (a bad marriage, an unwanted child, etc.). After describing my situation, Arnold looked at me and said "that is the most fucked up thing I have heard in a long time!" I immediately relaxed and felt tremendous empathy coming from Arnold. I felt that there was someone who would hear me and help me. I tended to be very competitive with Arnold during my group participation, sometimes being called a "junior therapist." He allowed me always to express my feelings without criticism while at the same time reminding me of my problems with authority (mother) and my constant need to be accepted and approved of. Many of my issues were anxiety based.

I had phobic reactions to situations out of my control and in one particular moment during a marathon while being held down I came to realize how important it was to allow a release from those phobic chains. Arnold was particularly loving and supportive and that night opened up an awakening that I am still working on today. Arnold was not afraid to interact during the group sessions and always seemed to grasp the specific needs of each of the members of the group. He was remarkable for his insights and I was amazed at his perceptive abilities.

Arnold had another characteristic that I found special, his honesty. He was not timid or circumspect about letting me and others know what he thought; he was not ever a "passive" participant – though careful not to interrupt or dominate with his point of view, he always tried to enlighten. He was patient with my defensiveness and resistance but always let me know what he thought at appropriate times. There were times during my therapy when I truly felt a

DOI: 10.4324/9781003391081-6

kind of love for him, though he was not that much older than I was, I definitely felt an affection for him as a father figure (more than I ever did for my own father). Like many people in therapy I was not particularly knowledgeable nor did I care about his "techniques" or "theoretical underpinnings" and like anyone seeking help, I was primarily interested in feeling better. Arnold's enormous gift of empathy and understanding was crucial for me in trusting him and his intentions. He was also very smart and during the marathon – courageous.

There was a time when I could not imagine not being in his care and to this day I know that my life since therapy and the success I have had are reflective of his being part of my life. Though I am still dealing with issues in my life (as are we all), I carry his work within me and believe that without a doubt he saved my life from the disaster it might have been. I am so pleased that Arnold is being honored, as few in his field are as deserving as he is. It is with love that I offer this to you.

Sincerely,
Alan Fishman

7 A Tribute to My Friend and Colleague Arnold Wm. Rachman, PhD

Henry Kellerman

Precursor

I felt a kinship with Dr. Arnold Wm. Rachman before I ever met him. It all began in the fall of 1964 when I applied to the psychoanalytic institute of the Postgraduate Center for Mental Health, in New York City, finding myself sitting across from the Dean of Admissions. I was accepted, but as a postscript the Dean said: "I'm also giving you one of the two National Institute of Mental Health Fellowships apportioned to our Postgraduate Center Psychoanalytic Institute. I gave the first one to that other genius, Rachman." Thus, all at once, Arnold and I together became labeled in a single sentence – and I report this accurately though immodest as that may seem.

And that's how the name "Rachman" entered my psyche, and to this day, more than a half century later, remains vividly etched.

Beginning History

Dr. Arnold William Rachman and I trained together in a class of twenty (10 evening and 10 daytime postgrad students). At first Arnold and I were casual friends/colleagues but then later became closer – so that now, in 2020, we are very good friends as well as special colleagues. Why special? The answer is that Arnold and I (both PhD psychologists and psychoanalysts) are the ones from our 1968 graduating class, along with Robert Marshall, PhD, (our other PhD psychologist and psychoanalyst classmate, good friend, and colleague) to have collectively published more material than any of the other classes of the Postgraduate Center's sixty-year year history. We three collectively have published as well as delivered papers at local, regional, and international conferences probably in the neighborhood of a couple of hundred or more of such publications and presentations, as well as having published collectively close to fifty books. In addition, the three of us meet the first Thursday of every month for dinner; we share things we're working on, and we shoot the breeze about this or that – and always at a different restaurant with each of us in turn choosing the restaurant. Existentially speaking, I believe each of us sees our monthly dinners as a happy and somewhat melancholy admixture. "Happy"

DOI: 10.4324/9781003391081-7

because we're sustaining a kind of hope that what we've done has been valuable and important and that we three are continuing our respective productive journeys. "Melancholy" because the three of us can look at the speeding future in the context of the incomprehensible past that has seemingly, and at the speed of light, become an interval to the present – and we look at it with a sense of reminiscence as well as with a sense of wonder at the growth experiences that became exceedingly important to our lives. I believe we three see this past as containing great advantage and we feel privileged to have had the opportunity for it. Yet, as is usually the case with the passing of time, it becomes difficult to fathom.

Preparing to write this chapter on Arnold Rachman, I did some research. First, the surname "Rachman" translates from the Hebrew into "merciful" or in the Yiddish version as Rakhmoness similarly meaning "sympathy," or in a vernacular sense, "pity." In addition, Arnold's mother's maiden surname was "Beispiel" (Sally Beispiel-Rachman-Grossman). In Yiddish, a beispiel is the word for being an *example* or a *model*; that is, meaning to be a standard of value in the sense of identifying something or someone who would be worthy of being useful as a model. I believe this is a suitable reference also to the concrete meaning of these characterizations as applied to Arnold Rachman's character – because he is certainly merciful, sympathetic, empathetic, and an example of someone to be admired, to be viewed and experienced as a model and, in addition, also to be seen as a mentor.

Thus, as to character, Arnold's involvement in his work reflects his egoism; that is, that egoism is defined as essentially to be comfortable and sure of what you're doing and to feel that what you're doing is valuable – especially in not particularly caring or worrying about what others are doing, and along with the sense that whatever others are doing could also be valuable – and finally not worrying about what others are thinking regarding what you are doing. This is to say that Arnold, is uncommonly selfless. In other words, Arnold does what he feels and knows is important.

In this case, the importance is in righting a wrong. More specifically, Arnold discovered Sándor Ferenczi and in the process he devoted enormous time and energy toward the objective of correcting a profound injustice regarding the issue of freedom of expression.

Thus, to this point, enter *Sándor Ferenczi: The Psychotherapist of Tenderness and Passion*, which is the title of Arnold's first published book on Ferenczi (Rachman, 1997); although for several years before writing this book on Ferenczi, he researched as much as he could on Ferenczi, and presented many papers in local, regional, and international conferences on the work and importance of Ferenczi.

So, the question becomes that in righting the wrong, why Ferenczi?

The answer to this question probably starts with archival history. This means a reference to Arnold's family emigrating from his Austrian-Hungarian Jewish heritage to America. As a first generation American, Arnold grew up in the southeast Bronx of New York City where he early on became aware of the "street." The street teaches many things, one of which is not to be shy or afraid of doing something that perhaps might go against the grain. Apparently, early on, Arnold learned the life-lesson that if it's important, pursue it because persistence is possibly the only real omnipotence.

So in thinking about "Why Ferenczi?," we need to continue to examine Arnold's life. In this sense, a bit later on Arnold struck gold at the *University of Chicago*. There at the University of Chicago is where Arnold found a vibration that matched the natural vibrations of his sensibilities regarding his very humanistic relational essence – so that, in turn, eventually when he finished his postdoctoral training (at the very eclectic psychodynamically oriented psychoanalytic institute of the *Postgraduate Center for Mental Health* in New York City – with its Freudian tinge), he knew that his professional internalized stance had a specific identity. Arnold emerged (born again, as it were) as that of a "relational psychotherapist."

University of Chicago and Legacy

At the University of Chicago it was the time of the late 1950s and early 1960s when, as a student there, Arnold was breathing in the relational atmosphere of Erika Fromm with her interest in the unconscious and in dream interpretation, Carl Rogers and his influential client-centered therapy, Saul Bellow in literature, Milton Friedman in economics, and Phillip Roth in literature (who are but a few selections of the unusual list of luminaries teaching then at the University of Chicago), and who in the years that Arnold attended the university were all swimming in and scrutinizing the world in a kind of – relational sensibility.

Therefore, when Arnold finally arrived at the Postgraduate Center for Mental Health, he was not arriving with the idea that the first best thing to have is an open mind. Rather, Arnold felt that the first best thing was to be interested in the consideration as to what was *in* that mind; that is, was it analytic as well as relational?

But that is still not going deep enough with respect to understanding something of essence in the Arnold William Rachman psyche. You see, in Yiddish speaking Eastern European Jewish culture resides a profound and ubiquitous value. It is a value that doesn't reach consciousness so that it is never specifically heard, and yet it remains a given in the unconscious and certainly noted in the very recesses of mind. No one actually says this, the "it," to children growing up in such a milieu.

The question is: What is this "it," this unspoken although ardent value?

Well, no child ever hears for example, a parent say: "*You must make a contribution!*" Thus, in this cross-section of Jewish culture the main issue is never solely about achievement. Of course, the quest for achievement is always in-the-air especially concerning academic excellence and/or in the investigation of new ideas such as inventions that could be of benefit to the greater good. In other words, it's not just that you must gain advantage because of achievement. No. Rather, it's that within the achievement motive (or under-pinning it) is that one must be concerned with doing something or giving oneself to something that is greater than the self.

Given this kind of deep cultural mandate, it is no wonder that a dispropor-tionate number of Nobel prize winners (as well as the Pulitzer in literature and the Field's medal in math) turn out to be Jewish (even in the face of anti-Semitic pressures). I'm sure that this Festschrift dedicated to Arnold is, in spirit, an equivalent honor.

Learning, achieving, contributing, loving, and living! This is the "big-five," – the essential five tools of the culture in which Arnold found himself – even found on the streets of the southeast Bronx. If a comparison were to be made with the language of baseball it would have to be said that Arnold Rachman has all five necessary power points (identified in baseball lingo as "power tools") in order to be great. In baseball these are: speed, power, hitting for average, fielding, and arm-strength).

I can personally attest to Arnold's ability in embracing his heritage of "con-tribution" in his academic, clinical, and research pursuits (in which he cer-tainly has had all five tools), but this is also true with respect to his baseball skills. You see, it was summer and, at one of the psychoanalytic retreat/confer-ences that we both attended at a beach resort, time was lagging so that sud-denly a spaldeen appeared (Bronxese for the Spalding brand). This spaldeen is a naked pink bouncing ball such as a tennis ball but without a fuzzy covering. So of all the forty or so people in our group that attended the retreat, both Arnold and I, knowing that each of us was from the streets of the southeast Bronx, the correct assumption we both independently then automatically made was that we both could play ball *well* and so we naturally started tossing the ball underhand to one another. We started throwing underhand to one another because we were not standing far apart. But as we took steps further away from one another the tossing became throwing and then the throwing and catching became more and more difficult the further we were apart because, as fate would have it, it was a windy day and the ball was a bit at the mercy of the insistent wind. Therefore, in order to catch the ball, one needed to be quite experienced in having such a required five-tool expertise.

Legacy

So in throwing like that, the ball is always directionally in a straight line. The straight line is important because it reflects accuracy. So how might this straight line apply to Arnold? Well, let's consider Arnold's professional legacy. Historically it begins with Freud but only in the sense that it was Freud who treated Ferenczi. Thus, with respect to honoring Arnold's cherished legacy, it really begins with Ferenczi straight line is, as Arnold put it in his book (Rachman, 1997, p. xi):

> *Ferenczi* analyzed *Clara Thompson*, who in turn analyzed *Lewis Wolberg*, in turn analyzed *Betty Feldman*, in turn analyzed *me*.

The straightest line is: Ferenczi to Thompson to Wolberg to Feldman to Rachman.

So now it's all about "contribution."

Contribution

"Contribution" is an important word for Arnold and he spotted it the first time he researched a Ferenczi article. This particular article by Ferenczi was highly significant to him.

Arnold's recollection of that moment is also described in his first book on *Sándor Ferenczi* noted above.

Arnold writes:

> I went to the library to look up Ferenczi's paper, with no special feeling that I was going to find anything of note. But when I began quickly to read, I felt an immediate rush of excitement. I was excited by the idea that at last, I was reading a psychoanalyst with whom I identify. Finally I had found a bridge between my training and education in humanistic psychotherapy and psychoanalysis, an experience I was awaiting all through my Analytic Institute training …. Examination of his three volumes of his *Contributions* convinced me that Ferenczi was a clinical genius, a significant figure in psychoanalysis, and a forgotten pioneer who deserved the attention of contemporary psychoanalysis.
>
> (pp. xiii–xiv)

And that's when Arnold says it became necessary "to right a wrong." Of course this reference refers to the wrong that was done to Ferenczi by Freud (and Jones) in partitioning Ferenczi from the mainstream of psychoanalysis – essentially exiling him. I could guess that Arnold experienced it as equivalent to a professional assassination – in street language, a rub-out. It became obvious that Ferenczi was no longer even discussed or read in mainstream psychoanalysis. Therefore, with respect to Arnold's heritage and sense of fairness and justice, it might not be a terribly difficult guess to make as to who was going to right that wrong?!

The Chronology of Arnold Wm. Rachman's Journey to Retrieve Ferenczi

At this point in Arnold's career his objective was clearly defined. In addition to attaining top-tier consulting, teaching, and supervising positions at various psychoanalytic institutes, and in addition to his private practice as a psycho-analytic relational psychotherapist, a newer title was added to his profile – that of: "*Scholar in the history of psychoanalysis*," perhaps first identified by this writer in the volume: *Dictionary of Psychopathology* (Kellerman, 2009, p. 206). It was absolutely important to include Arnold as a separate entry in this dictionary, especially since a detailed history of the ins and outs of the fascinating history of psychoanalysis is beautifully uncovered, traced, and eloquently rendered in his book on Ferenczi.

It needs to be understood that Ferenczi's exile was, in the ongoing history of psychoanalysis, equivalent to his death. Arnold, as well as a few others who in a sense mourned this so-called death, mourned it the way anyone mourns – that is, along with attendant behavior such as crying and suffering. I'm guessing that Arnold didn't cry, but for sure he suffered the injustice correspondingly suffered by Ferenczi. Further, mourning and crying is putatively seen in psycho-analytic understanding (and from a deeply unconscious need) to mean that the entire mourning process is an attempt at *retrieval of the lost object*. The tragedy of loss is that the psyche wants to deny it, to isolate it, and to not need to suffer it. Therefore, the diagnosis to such loss is frequently *reactive depression*. In a reactive depression the depression is designed in the psyche to allay, at least temporarily, the intense anxiety or trauma of the realization of the loss.

In a way I would say that the only thing that rescued Arnold from this sort of depression over the exile-death of Ferenczi from the entire exciting psycho-analytic universe was Arnold's determination and indignance – actually his anger over this injustice. So instead of mourning and feeling disempowered – that is, actually possibly isomorphically identifying with Ferenczi's ouster and corresponding disempowerment, Yes, instead, Arnold got angry. He got angry because anger is always a re-empowerment. He didn't want Ferenczi to be disempowered nor did he himself want to be disempowered. He wanted Ferenczi to be empowered, to be heard and to be reintroduced into the psy-choanalytic mainstream as one of many voices. He wanted Ferenczi retrieved!

So what did Dr. Arnold Rachman do?

Deeds

It started with Dr. Hannah Kapit, a senior supervisor, lecturer, and training analyst at the Postgraduate Center. Dr. Kapit was a personal friend of Margaret Severn, Elizabeth Severn's daughter. Elizabeth Severn was a woman with whom Ferenczi would conduct what he defined as a *mutual analysis*. In this sense, the analyst's personality became, as Arnold states: "integral to the ana-lytic process." Severn helped Ferenczi formulate his trauma theory of neurosis and the relaxation method "to deal with it" (Rachman, 1997, p. 373). In addi-tion, Severn became important because, in their treatment together, Arnold states that Ferenczi needed, because of this new patient-centered psychother-apy, to forgo issues of power, control, and status (p. 407). Therefore, Arnold makes clear that Severn was and is an important figure in the life of Ferenczi as well as in the life of the history of psychoanalysis.

So, parenthetically, what did Arnold then do? Of course, predictably, piece by piece he researched the life of Severn and then wrote the book entitled: *Elizabeth Severn: The "Evil" Genius of Psychoanalysis* (Rachman, 2018).

In the meantime, Arnold was contacted by Dr. Kapit who of course knew of Arnold's focus on Ferenczi, and who told Arnold that she was contacted by a Peter Lipskis, the executor of the Elizabeth Severn papers and that these papers were in the possession of Severn's daughter, Margaret Severn. The issue of possible purchase of the papers was discussed and apparently their location was identified as in the possession of Margaret who lived in Vancouver, British Columbia. Several other steps were taken and before anyone knew it, Arnold was on his way to Vancouver. Arnold purchased the Severn archive.

The question was where to store this treasure-trove. Without hesitation Arnold was in touch with Dr. Nellie Thompson, archivist of the A. A. Brill Library of the internationally prestigious *New York Psychoanalytic Institute*. Dr. Thompson was extremely helpful and agreed to temporarily store the Severn boxes of papers at the Library. In the meantime, Arnold searched for a more permanent home for the archive and finally discussed it all with Dr. Leonard Bruno, Head, Scientific Manuscript Division, *The Library of Congress*, Washington, D.C. Mr. Bruno invited Arnold to deliver a lecture at the Library of Congress on the Severn collection which Arnold gratefully did. Then under Dr. Leonard Bruno and Dr. James Hutson, Chief, Manuscript Division, the Elizabeth Severn section was established along with the Sándor Ferenczi section – as sections of the Sigmund Freud archive.

But Arnold was not finished. He was then instrumental, along with Dr. Judith Mészáros, President, *The Sándor Ferenczi Society*, and co-founder, *The Sándor Ferenczi House*, Budapest, Hungary, in having an Elizabeth Severn section incorporated into the *Sándor Ferenczi House* in Budapest. It was then, at that time, about twenty years or so since Arnold first stumbled upon Ferenczi – of course in a library – at the library of the *Postgraduate Center for Mental Health*. We need here to understand that we're talking about Arnold Wm. Rachman, so obviously there is much more to come, more books to write, and more lectures to present. Arnold's focus is an example of serious thinking, serious expenditure of energy, courage, and a zeal toward making a contribution – an investment and interest that was and is greater than the self.

Arnold, my friend, you are heroic even to those who don't particularly define themselves as Ferenczians. However, again, it is universally recognized that you've done something singularly important. You did in fact, retrieve Ferenczi. You brought him back!

A yahsher koiakh dir, mine frynt, Arnold. (In transliteration, a Hebrew expression used in Yiddish – meaning: More power to you, Arnold, my friend.)

Further, to have been invited to participate in this Festschrift organized in your honor, Arnold, has been a pleasure for me and I'm happy to have been invited. It was for me an overdetermined moment – a chance also to contribute.

References

Kellerman, H. *Dictionary of Psychopathology*. New York: Columbia University Press, 2009.

Rachman, A. W. *Sándor Ferenczi: The Psychotherapist of Tenderness and Passion*. Northvale, NJ: Jason Aronson, 1997.

Rachman, A. W. *Elizabeth Severn: The "Evil" Genius of Psychoanalysis*. London: Routledge, 2018.

8 A Loving Tribute from an Analysand and Friend

Robert E. Kennedy

I met Arnold Rachman by happenstance. In September 1978 I began a three-year program at the Blanton-Peale Institute of Mental Health in New York City. As an essential part of that program, I was required to undergo my own analysis with one, not of our own faculty. Since I was a Jesuit Catholic priest and committed to celibate life, one of my teachers suggested that I should be analyzed by a woman. I had already decided that I wanted to be analyzed by a Jew because I wanted someone from a world and language different from my own who would challenge me at every turn of the road.

So, I looked for a Jewish woman analyst and called Edrita Fried but she said she was too busy to see me. A friend told me to call Arnold. I did call Arnold, and he responded at once. We talked for an hour, and I decided to go with him. We began our work three times a week and after the first year, Arnold introduced me to group therapy that included several Jewish women, so I found what I was looking for after all.

During that first meeting, I made only one request of Arnold – that he be responsive to me. I did not want to talk to an empty chair. Arnold assured me he would be responsive, and he was. When I spoke with him of the trauma of the Irish people to centuries-long military occupation and of the famine in which one million people starved to death, Arnold listened most sympathetically.

And then, in what he later called judicious self-disclosure on the part of the analyst, Arnold spoke of his love for his Austrian-Jewish heritage, of the tears he shed in a Holocaust Museum, and of his sensitivity to Jewish trauma in American life. We grieved together in what he later called mutual analysis on behalf of the analysand.

It was in large part because of Arnold that I accompanied a group of Zen teachers and students to visit Auschwitz-Birkenau in 1999. I spent a week there in the November cold and rainy walking from the train station to the barracks to the gas chamber to the ash pit in the footsteps of so many victims. We did not hurry but spent hours in each place without eating or drinking in remembrance of those who suffered and starved there. Arnold called this trip the role of active measures in the analysis of trauma. Talking in his office was

DOI: 10.4324/9781003391081-8

not enough to break open the heart, but go and see and touch and feel, be present and hear their cry.

Another experience that shaped my life in those years with Arnold was the work of Sándor Ferenczi. Ferenczi, as Arnold revealed him to me by word and example, was a romantic and imaginative man creative in his thinking and warm and empathetic in his relations with analysands. This compassionate attitude was far removed from the image of analysts of his own day, silent, remote, and note-taking. On the contrary, his analytic approach was full of tenderness and passion.

From my own experience, Arnold lived out in his professional life what he loved in Ferenczi. His analysis did not end at the end of the therapeutic hour. He journeyed to the Bronx to attend my installation as a Catholic Zen teacher. He came to Fordham University the evening I led a program in Catholicism and sexuality. He offered to contribute financially to an interreligious group of teachers, rabbis, and priests who were living and sleeping on the street with the homeless. He and Nancy invited me to dinner to celebrate my honorary degree from Holy Cross College. He came with a gift to celebrate my 80th birthday. He made extra time to sit with me at the death of a woman who was a lifelong friend. Arnold became what he loved in Ferenczi – an analyst of tenderness and compassion.

There are two events in my years with Arnold that I would like to share with you that reveal something about Arnold's character. One event was the night he invited me to go to Madison Square Garden with him to see the Knicks play. It was a long night and Arnold looked very tired. He had recently been in a car crash that left him broken in his body and blind in one eye. I thought he was going to tell me that he was giving up his practice and retiring. Not a bit of it! He told me he was about to be married and invited me to the wedding. I was stunned by this force of life and love that radiated from him when he had every excuse to slow down and give up. His lived example that night was unforgettable.

Another example of Arnold's responsiveness to life and to me occurred one afternoon in his office when our therapy hour was winding down. I mentioned to Arnold that Thomas Mann in *The Magic Mountain* had written the best description of analysis I had ever read. Arnold said, "read it to me." Mann wrote:

> Analysis as an instrument of enlightenment and civilization is good, in so far as it shatters absurd convictions, acts as a solvent upon natural preferences, and undermines authority; good in other words in that it sets free, refines, humanizes, makes slaves ripe for freedom.

Arnold sat straight up in his chair, reached for his pen, and said, "wonderful, read it to me again and slowly." He was always willing to learn, think new, and rewrite everything. My formal analysis with Arnold ended thirty years ago but of course, it never completely ended. I still see him now and then to keep my limitations from spilling out on my students and friends. But I also visit him again to experience his warm welcome and the joy of being known and loved.

Robert E. Kennedy, S.J., PhD
Professor Emeritus
St. Peter's University
Jersey City, NJ

9 A Reflection on My Relationship with Arnold Rachman, PhD and His Contributions to the Revival of the Lost Legacy of Sándor Ferenczi

Susan A. Klett

Arnold Rachman, a cherished colleague and co-author, is a world-renowned Ferenczi scholar who has contributed to The Ferenczi Renaissance for over forty years. I met Arnold for the first time when he was invited by The Postgraduate Psychoanalytic Society to lecture on Sándor Ferenczi (2008) in the Oak Room of Baruch College where we housed our library. He is a tall man of Austrian Hungarian Jewish Heritage who spoke with passion and an in-depth knowledge on Sándor Ferenczi. His respect for, identification with, and devotion to Ferenczi was palpable. I recall attending a psychoanalytic theatrical performance "The Freud/Ferenczi Letters: A Staged Reading of Selected Letters" with Arnold Rachman (a relational psychoanalyst) in the role of Ferenczi and Elliot Adler (A Freudian analyst) in the role of Freud. When the room opened to the audience for discussion, a Freudian scholar shouted "Ferenczi is not a real psychoanalyst, he performed wild analysis." Arnold's response was strong and swift, mirroring the heated dialogue on stage. The audience was stunned. Many believed that this was a staged continuation of the play; staged it was not, but reflective of Arnold's protection of Ferenczi's reputation and his frustration with rigid thinkers – psychoanalysts who excluded and devalued other theorists. Like Ferenczi, Arnold is empathic, open minded, courageous, and creative. Through his meticulous psycho-historical research, his lectures, his in-depth analysis of Ferenczi's clinical cases, and his contribution of the letters, photos, and personal notes of Elizabeth Severn to the archives of the Library of Congress, he continues to be a dynamic force in reclaiming Sándor Ferenczi's place in psychoanalytic history.

One of Arnold's most courageous stances has been his championing of Ferenczi for his courage and intricate work on the development of a trauma theory based upon his groundbreaking paper "Confusion of the Tongues between the Adult and the Child: The Language of Tenderness and of Passion" (1949). Rachman's determination for justice in uncovering and exposing the silencing of Ferenczi's most important contribution is parallel to Ferenczi's attempts at uncovering and exposing the silencing of victims of sexual abuse and incest trauma. The power of patriarchy is evident today as we hear the voices of those silenced for years joining together in the "Me Too" movement, exposing the prevalence of sexual abuse by those in positions of power within

DOI: 10.4324/9781003391081-9

families and throughout every social and political structure. The injuries suffered by these victims have been acknowledged and the perpetrators are beginning to be held accountable for their crimes. Arnold and I have found Ferenczi's trauma theory to be instrumental for understanding and effectively treating victims of sexual abuse and incest trauma, which we have demonstrated through numerous case illustrations in our book *Analysis of the Incest Trauma: Retrieval, Recovery, Renewal* (2015).

It is a pleasure and honor to acknowledge Arnold Rachman, a warm and generous intellectual who continues to dedicate his professional life and enormous energy to teaching and writing about the life and work of Sándor Ferenczi. Presently, Arnold is in the process of completing two books, soon to be published, and collaborating on four others while he makes time to swim daily. I am impressed with the close friendships he has developed and maintained with colleagues, both nationally and internationally; many have deepened over the course of fifty years. Arnold is the person who shows up. For example, I have sat in rooms with him for the memorials of too many of our mutual friends/colleagues. When I was recognizing Henry Kellerman, PhD, for his body of work and asked who he would like to acknowledge him, he was quick to list Arnold as one of his best friends. At the time Arnold was living in Florida; however, he immediately responded to my request and we found a way to have him in the room through speakerphone. When Arnold was a speaker in the Plenary Session at the International Ferenczi Conference "Faces of Trauma" held in Budapest (2012) he was surrounded by friends and colleagues. Throughout the week presentations were going on simultaneously in many rooms. When I was preparing to speak, Arnold entered the room; I appreciated his interest and support. It was Arnold's presentation on Ferenczi in 2008 that inspired me. His enthusiasm was contagious and led to my avidly reading all of his journal and book publications on Ferenczi, which profoundly influenced my psychoanalytic work with severely traumatized patients.

Today Ferenczi stands alongside Sigmund Freud as a significant figure in the evolution of psychoanalysis. Rachman's passionate and relentless works (1997a, 1997b, 1997c, 1998a, 1998b, 2003, 2007, 2010) shed light upon Ferenczi's original concepts and techniques, which were expanded upon and incorporated into self-psychology, the British middle-school, and relational and contemporary theories.

Arnold Rachman's prolific writings, teachings, and lectures have awakened many mental health clinicians to the depth and breadth of Sándor Ferenczi's contributions to self-psychology, object relations, and relational and contemporary psychoanalytic theories. While I was aware of Ferenczi's writing on language and the body, as well as his famous Confusion of Tongues Trauma Theory and the tragedy of its suppression for many years, I was not aware that various concepts and techniques at the core of contemporary theory building had originated with Ferenczi. Arnold Rachman's rigorous investigations helped to claim Sándor Ferenczi's place in psychoanalytic history, not only by exposing his erasure following the Confusion of Tongues' paper, but by linking present contemporary theories to their origins as developed within the case studies of Sándor Ferenczi.

References

Ferenczi, S. Confusion of the tongues between the adults and the child: The language of tenderness and of passion, *International Journal of Psychoanalysis*, 33: 225–230, 1949.

Rachman, A.W. *Sándor Ferenczi: The Psychotherapist of Tenderness and Passion*. Northvale, NJ: Jason Aronson, 1997a.

Rachman, A.W. The suppression and censorship of Ferenczi's confusion of tongues paper, *Psychoanalytic Inquiry*, 17(4): 459–485, 1997b.

Rachman, A.W. Chapter 21 Sándor Ferenczi and the evolution of a self psychology: Framework in psychoanalysis, *Progress in Self Psychology*, 13: 341–365, 1997c.

Rachman, A.W. Ferenczi's relaxation principle and the issue of therapeutic responsiveness, *American Journal of Psychoanalysis*, 58(1): 63–81, 1998a.

Rachman, A.W. Judicious self-disclosure by the psychoanalysis, *International Forum of Psychoanalysis*, 7(4): 263–269, 1998b.

Rachman, A.W. *Psychotherapy of Difficult Cases: Flexibility and Responsiveness in Contemporary Practice*. Madison, CT: Psychosocial Press, 2003.

Rachman, A. W. Sándor Ferenczi's contributions to the evolution of psychoanalysis, *Psychoanalytic Psychology*, 24(1): 74–96, 2007.

Rachman, A.W. The origins of a relational perspective in the ideas of Sándor Ferenczi: The Budapest School of Psychoanalysis, *Psychoanalytic Perspectives*, 7(1): 43–60, 2010.

Rachman, A.W. and Klett, S.A. *Analysis of the Incest Trauma: Retrieval, Recovery, Renewal*. London: Karnac, 2015.

10 Arnold Rachman, an Unsung Hero

Harold Kooden

Opening Statement

It is an honor to write this essay as I feel that Arnold is now receiving his long-deserved recognition as one of the central figures in the changing face of psychoanalysis and psychotherapy. Since Arnold and I have known each other for almost sixty years, dating back to when we were fellow students, I have a broad range of experiences to comment on. Clearly, other essays in this Festschrift will have a depth in their contribution specific to their area of contact with Arnold. What I, as a white, gay man, want to share with you is the breadth of our history as well as a fuller picture of the man we are all honoring.

Fellow Classmate

We met in the early 1960s while we were both in the Committee on Human Development (HD), an interdisciplinary program at the University of Chicago. HD stressed that a person was to be studied as a psychological being living in a physical body in a culture/social environment with all these components interacting. (Intersectionality was not yet a common word.) Sociology, anthropology, biology, embryology, and genetics were studied as well as specific HD courses that covered childhood, adolescence, adulthood, and old age. In fact, one of our professors began what became the national field of gerontology. We also learned how to conduct and analyze a variety of research methodologies and understand their limits and flaws. HD also stressed the study of social systems, whether they be a family, group, or societal. The Clinical Psychology and Testing program was another requirement for those of us who wanted to become clinical psychologists. HD was also in total contrast to the Psychology Department, which was very traditional in its coursework and attitudes, as well as none of the faculty or students were people of color and openly gay students were expelled. The Counseling Center, founded by Carl Rogers, was also available to us for our practicums and clinical work. HD and the Counseling Center are central to this Festschrift in their relevance to Arnold's philosophy, practice, and research. HD taught us how to analyze

DOI: 10.4324/9781003391081-10

and think "outside the box" and never lose sight of all the many influences on human development and behavior. It presented us with a variety of theories and research underpinning the philosophical approach on how to fully understand the total person. The Counseling Center taught us how to listen to the client's statements and understand their experiences, which was the principle component of the healing process. We were taught how to listen with all our senses and not just the intellect, so that the client was affirmed by someone truly listening to their story. As you the reader will see, this background is integral to understanding Arnold's uniqueness and the depth of his commitment to his beliefs.

Personal Friend

Being a life-time friend and living in the same city has given me the opportunity of experiencing Arnold in a variety of situations. I can easily say he has become the loving, older brother that I never had. Knowing him from a time before his children were born, I have seen him as the devoted and caring father and grandfather who fully accepted all the responsibility of these roles. His children's best interests were always paramount for him, though, in my estimation, he did not pay enough attention to his own needs. This loving quality extended to his loyalty in friendships as well. As a gay man, I was initially amazed to see his comfort with me and his reaching out to maintain our relationship as a respectful peer. Because of my own hangups, I put up many barriers to deepening our relationship but he continued to reach out and show his interest in my life. He and his wife were at my wedding to my husband. His love for me also included his ability to express his negative feelings about and with me as well! He has shown me the deepest meaning of a true friendship, whereby I became part of his extended family. Not only is he capable of having both female and male friends, he sees these friendships as part of his emotional support system. What has impressed me about his friendships is the equality and lack of hierarchy in them. I had the honor of being his best man at his wedding, which, to me, was not only a measure of our feelings for each other but also his statement to his family and friends about whom he considered his best friend.

Professional Colleague

Though we talked about intimate details of our lives, we never talked about professional issues until the last decade. Ours was basically a social relationship though we were in the same profession. He went through his psychoanalytic training to become a psychoanalyst and then training analyst. My path was initially through community mental health and activism within the health and mental health field. I then began to focus on psychological and psychotherapeutic issues for lesbians and gay men. It was interesting that both of us became instrumental in making significant changes in psychology and psychotherapy through our respective activities. Luckily, through my social and professional network, I knew about how he worked with gay men as clients and I was impressed. This was at a time when homosexuality was still considered a mental illness by many therapists. Eventually, as I read some of his professional papers, I understood better how he could be so comfortable and supportive of gay men; he thought outside the box. He was capable of seeing what was the best way to be supportive of his clients and be willing to risk taking unusual steps to doing what he felt was best for his clients. This perceptive ability of his became more evident to me when he and I started working together professionally in our mutual analysis. I have also been at professional meetings where he has presented his research, i.e., university and psychoanalytic training programs, Library of Congress, etc.

Mutual Analysis

About four years ago, when Arnold was living in Miami and we only had telephone contact, he proposed that we start engaging in a mutual analysis. He defined it as a commitment to a weekly conversation in which, besides talking about our lives, we would both act as each other's therapist. This process began because we both trusted each other and were willing to make significant changes in our lives. Once Arnold and his wife moved back to New York City, this became a weekly, two-hour session. Mutual analysis is relevant to this Festschrift as it validates a significant facet of Arnold that others have seen from other contexts – his persistence in growing, making changes when necessary and, despite opposition, courage in defending his positions. Our sessions were free-flowing; sometimes catch-up, sometimes therapy, and, significantly, sometimes helping Arnold edit his working manuscripts from his current projects. (As you will see in the next section, this editing work is relevant as it gave me more insight into some of Arnold's strengths in working with clients.) Mutual analysis indicated to me that Arnold could be comfortable in a therapeutic relationship in which he did not have a one-sided position of authority. Given that I already knew an ex-client of his and I have listened to the way Arnold talked and wrote about his clients, his absence of a need for a hierarchical, power relationship as therapist is further evidence of the consistency of his actions as a therapist and of his landmark writings. Both of us have had transformative experiences in our mutual analysis in which healing of trauma has taken place. Though I believe that friendship is not a requirement for mutual analysis, I have experienced a deepening of our friendship that reflects back on Arnold's willingness to be vulnerable and take emotional risks with a friend. One of these risks is being able to express openly both positive and negative feelings about each other without making it an attack or fault-finding. Therefore, this mutual analysis has shown me that Arnold's ability to hear another person's perspective without judgment or defensiveness is another of his special qualities.

Co-editing

You may wonder why I have put "co-editing" as a separate section. I have done this as I have observed a distinct ability of Arnold's that is reflected in his functioning as a therapist both to me and, by inference, to others. I am co-editing a book with Arnold about the different paths men and women have taken to becoming psychoanalysts and/or psychotherapists. I have read all the essays, including my own, to which Arnold has made editorial suggestions as to making these better essays. Though I did not like the idea of rewriting my own essay, I knew that Arnold's suggestions would result in a much better essay. He had zeroed in on exactly what was lacking in my essay, which was an integration of two different kinds of professional experience with all my accompanying theoretical underpinnings. Though the other essays were very different in terms of writing styles and life experiences, he was able to approach them similarly as to what would make them better essays. He was able to see the unique qualities of each essay and the writer's experience and then communicate what would be the next step to make it a more meaningful essay. I was very impressed with this ability of his as an editor. Combining this observation with my own experience in mutual analysis with him, I could easily infer that this was a very noteworthy ability that he had as a therapist – being able to see the next step that his client needed to take for further development. He was capable of listening to the client's experience (story) and take the client further in the therapeutic process. He could bring all his intellect, feelings, and expertise into this process, but the direction was determined by his careful listening to the client and not coming from an imposition of another theoretical position. In other words, Arnold demonstrates the ability to listen to the core of the person in front of him and, as we know, being heard is essential for therapeutic progress.

Sándor Ferenczi and Elizabeth Severn

Given Arnold's experiences at the University of Chicago, it is easy to understand his groundbreaking and passionate commitment to Ferenczi and his work. The Committee on Human Development taught him to question accepted dogma and to think creatively. We were rewarded for thinking "outside the box" and for pursuing our dreams. At the Counseling Center, he was exposed to a unique kind of relationship with his clients and how to listen with his heart. All this came into conflict when he began his psychoanalytic training, which followed a much more traditional path. At that time in the 1960s, Ferenczi was absent from the training program and Arnold accidentally discovered him – a discovery that was to change his life. He began to see a possibility that he could still stay within the realm of psychoanalysis and legitimately incorporate a more humanistic approach. Arnold's uniqueness is that he did not take the more typical path of creating "a new theory and school of psychotherapy." He saw that Ferenczi had been written out of psychoanalytic history by both Freud and his followers; his goal was to prove that Ferenczi's ideas rightfully were a corrective expansion of psychoanalytic theory and practice. In his pursuit, he also traced the important influence of Elizabeth Severn on Ferenczi's thinking and practice. As will be seen in future publications, he has unearthed significant information which also puts her into her rightful place in the history of psychoanalysis. Though Ferenczi was not forgotten in Europe and Hungary has its own Ferenczi society which sup-ported a "local son," this kind of support was absent in the United States when Arnold began his life-time research. This really was a revolutionary position, since in the United States Ferenczi had either been written out or relegated to a very negative position. Arnold was willing to be a risk-taker and fight for what he felt was a different kind of truth. I experienced Arnold's gen-uine humility in all this work – he was not doing it for personal glory or career advancement. He simply wanted to get this positive message out there and bring Ferenczi and Severn into any meaningful discussion of psychoanalysis and practice. As he had learned to bring his heart into the therapeutic pro-cess, he brought his own heart into the Ferenczi/Severn research to which he has dedicated his life.

Therapeutic Orientation and Practice

Significantly, Arnold struggled to incorporate his beliefs and discoveries into his practice as a psychoanalyst. As I have said before, he did not try to create a "new field or a new psychological theory." He wanted to expand psychoa-nalysis beyond an endeavor only of the analyst's intellect and skill in analyz-ing. His years of training showed him the limitations of this approach. Through many "trials and tribulations," he became convinced that the analyst is to be a "therapeutic presence" who generously listens to the life story of the person in front of him. Feeling heard is, in and of itself, a healing experience. Arnold strongly believes that though it is difficult to teach "how to be a therapeutic presence," it is essential for becoming a healer. It is no wonder that Arnold is especially skilled in dealing with childhood trauma since the trauma must be fully experienced and heard to begin the healing process towards wholeness. Arnold has shown that, in spite of an extensive background in psychological theory, he does not impose this on the client – he lets the client's needs dictate his clinical actions. He is comfortable "not being in charge," but always being present. His writings have also shown that he is not afraid to use his intuition in taking creative, psychotherapeutic actions. As I have stated before, my experience with him as co-editor tells me that he has an uncanny ability to listen and sense what is the next best step. I also experienced this in our mutual analysis. Whether by direct experience and/or inference, the previous sections of this Festschrift support what I am saying about Arnold as a master therapist – he is the healing presence.

Concluding Statement

Having known Arnold for such a long time and over a variety of situations, I feel free to lovingly lavish praise on him. I would conjecture that if becoming an analyst had not been available to him, he might have become a rabbi. He is such a perfect example of the Jewish tradition of "Tikkun Olam" – repairing (healing) the part of the world that touches you. Clearly, his whole life has been dedicated to the healing process, whether in his personal relationships, his therapy, or his writings. He has been courageous in holding to his heartfelt beliefs, though this has brought conflict and an outlier status. In spite of the national and international transformative effects of his work, he is humble about what he has done. I have joked with him about his lack of competitiveness, which sometimes makes him unaware of how competitive and power-hungry others are. I am so pleased that Arnold will now have a chance to read the praises that others are giving him. His genuine guilelessness and humility have, in the past, prevented him from seeing the scope of what he has done. I feel that he has now evolved in seeing and appreciating what he has accomplished and who he has become. It is a privilege to contribute to this Festschrift on honoring Arnold Rachman.

11 For Arnold Rachman

In Appreciation of his Courage, Leadership, and Sensitivity for the Humanity in Us All

Joseph Lichtenberg

People who share a common interest, especially an admired common interest, find it easy to find compatibility. So, it has been with Arnold Rachman and me with respect to Sándor Ferenczi. We have come to our interest, even fascination with the Hungarian psychoanalyst's favorite son of Freud through different experiences.

Arnold states,

> I have wanted to write about my journey in finding Ferenczi and his importance for my development as a psychoanalyst. My struggles cover a journey from phenomenology to Humanistic Psychotherapy to Relational Analysis, which covers the time period in psychoanalysis of roughly 1960 to the 1980s. I found it difficult to develop an identity as a psychoanalyst until I discovered Ferenczi. His two-person psychology helped me incorporate the interpersonal encounter, intersubjectivity, clinical flexibility, responsiveness, and empathy.

My journey was mediated by my mentor, model, and sponsor Lewis Hill. Lewis was a prominent psychoanalytic leader and former president of the American Psychoanalytic Association. When I knew him he had given up private practice, recovering from alcoholism, and become director of training at the Sheppard and Pratt Hospital in Baltimore. As a young psychiatrist, Lewis had gone to Hungary to spend a summer in analysis with Ferenczi. On his return, he entered analysis with Clara Thompson. Lewis tells the story of a Ferenczi-like human-to-human exchange with her. On one occasion Thompson asked him why was he so uncharacteristically quiet – what was on his mind. Lewis reluctantly answered that he was bothered by the sight of her legs – they were so fat. She responded, "Yes they are and if you know anything I can do about it let me know." It was Clara Thompson who had sat on Ferenczi's lap and famously wrote in a letter, "I am allowed to kiss Papa Ferenczi, as often as I like."

I was trained to be guided in my psychoanalytic endeavors by neutrality, abstinence, and anonymity in order to guarantee the analysand's associations and intrapsychic structures were not being influenced by other than

DOI: 10.4324/9781003391081-11

interpretation and insight. The Ferenczi legacy that drew Arnold and me to Ferenczi and to each other was that a patient is not a petri dish we are worried about contaminating. Our patients are human beings with whom, as analysts, we establish an intersubjective relatedness that facilitates the emergence of the patient's often painful guilt and/or shaming, feelings, intentions, and goals. We enter where the confusion of tongues between parent and child has left a patient with maladaptive patterns of relating, striving, and physiological regulation. Arnold describes ways in which the Confusion of Tongues was significant. Particularly damaging is the affect of confusion, the domination associated with seduction and abuse, the accommodation of the victim, and identification with the aggressor. We must go with the patient into his regressive state and re-experience of trauma. "What such neurotics need is really to be adopted and to partake for the first time in their lives of the advantages of a normal nursery." What Ferenczi is advocating here is not the indulgence of a good-natured mother-analyst, but the gradual development by trial and error of a new choreography (Arnold's word) of the analyst–analysand interaction in the treatment.

When Arnold discovered Ferenczi, he was blown away by Ferenczi's theory and application of it. He also discovered that scattered all over the world were adherents like André Haynal, Michael Balint, and Lewis Aron as well as others who gave no credit to Ferenczi like Carl Rogers. So he became the organizer of a revival and restoration. He issued a rallying call for appreciation of the humanistic quality of mutual involvement and mutual respect between patient and therapist, Ferenczi's bridge between relational analysis and phenomenologic and humanistic psychotherapy. Parallel and independently in the United States, Sullivan was advocating something similar. Klein, Lacan, and Bion and ego psychology were going off in different directions from Ferenczi and each other. Under Arnold's leadership, adherents of Ferenczi held their own and gained increasing respect for the intersubjective sharing that focused on self under Kohut. Our field owes Arnold a debt of gratitude for his leadership, his pulling together analysts from all over the world to share their application of the Ferenczi spirit to a variety of clinical problems. An honor that Lew Aron and I participated in was Arnold's being invited to present a discussion of Ferenczi to the Library of Congress. Another unique outcome of Arnold's leadership is the two volumes of *Psychoanalytic Inquiry*. There was so much to say that the original issue on Ferenczi's legacy in 1997 was followed by an issue on innovations in theory and technique in 2014.

Along with his huge effort to revitalize Ferenczi's achievements, Arnold was not finished with being a rescuer of lost reputations. His next subject for rescue, Elizabeth Severn, was a more difficult "case." She had been regarded as the malignant person who pulled Ferenczi into non-analytic practices and in the process ruined his health. Elizabeth Severn, in Arnold's reconstruction of history, is regarded as an intelligent creative collaborator of Ferenczi's expansion of technique and theory of trauma.

It was in the eight-year analysis of Elizabeth Severn that Ferenczi demonstrated those creative qualities as a person and clinician that I so admired. He showed remarkable dedication to helping Severn overcome her severe emotional problems; knowingly accepting an analysand who had a history of severe childhood traumas and a lifetime of unsuccessful attempts at therapy. Ferenczi acted like a loving and empathic parent who would do whatever was necessary to heal his sick child. He used the analytic encounter as a laboratory to research, treat, and understand trauma. He extended the boundaries of the analytic encounter by listening to what Severn was experiencing in their relationship and what she felt was needed to make it fully therapeutic.

No one in the history of psychoanalysis had ever before engaged an analysand so fully that he/she became a co-creator of the analytic encounter. It took qualities of emotional honesty, fearless self-examination, elasticizing personal and professional boundaries, a renunciation of status and authority needs, and willingness for confronting his own emotional issues.

Ferenczi pioneered the emotionally active analyst, rather than the analyst as a cognitive interpreter in a sterile field who is performing analytic surgery. His emotional courage, daring, and capacity to deviate from established tradition, while maintaining a connection to the core of analytic theory and technique has provided me with the role model for being a meaningful dissident.

Finally, I wish to say that, like Sándor Ferenczi, Arnold Rachman is an analyst/caregiver who does what it takes to help their analysands and students – an analyst/caregiver who has, and respects in others, the courage to challenge orthodoxy and explore in the search for a better way.

12 Festschrift for Arnold Wm. Rachman

"Great, Great, Grandson" of Sándor Ferenczi

Robert J. Marshall

Personal and Collegial

It is with great pleasure that I write a tribute for Arnold. I have known Arnold since we began our training at the Postgraduate Center for Mental Health (PGCMH) nearly sixty years ago. Because of his openness and friendliness, we immediately began sharing our thoughts and feelings about our families and bonded in our mutual struggles with the Dean of Training. From a personal point of view, I admired his frankness and affability, as well as his hearty laughter. From a professional perspective, I was impressed with his humanistic point of view, his regard for Erik Erikson, and his Rogerian, client-centered orientation of the Chicago school, whereas I had been exposed to a more psychoanalytic and "scientist-clinician" training.

We became more connected in a two-semester class on group therapy conducted by Asya Kadis, a brilliant group analyst. In the first session Asa took the roll, sat back and said nothing. Besides checking the attendance, she uttered not one word for the next twelve sessions while sitting in her chair slightly bobbing and weaving. The varied emotional reactions of the twelve candidates over the semester was astounding. Candidates wept, shouted, begged, or lapsed into silence. In this setting and in the next semester when Asa participated in analyzing our reaction to her silence, I realized what a feeling person was Arnold. I recall that he was the leading spokesman for the bewilderment, anger, chagrin, and diverse feelings induced by Asa's silence and eventual analysis of our emotional reactions. I discovered his capacity for passion, empathy, and understanding. To this day I stand in awe of the range of his feelings, his ability to freely verbalize his feelings, and his capacity for assuming the emotional leadership of the group. The power of that year's work led to all group members, save one, joining the Group Therapy Certificate program.

Throughout our training at PGCMH, I noted that Arnold and a couple of his cohorts were outspoken about any defects or injustices in the program. For example, in a free-floating course about Freud, Arnold asked for and received a more structured presentation. When the students were required to take a course in psychoanalytic consultation in the community, Arnold and others

DOI: 10.4324/9781003391081-12

questioned the rationale for taking us away from clinical psychoanalysis. Arnold was among the most candid about professors who were inadequate in the content and presentation of the course material. He was also intolerant of teachers who were authoritarian in their presentation. In retrospect, Arnold was manifesting Ferenczi-like characteristics.

PGCMH, led by Lewis Wolberg, was known for its eclectic program with a heavy emphasis on Freud, led by graduates of the New York Psychoanalytic Institute, but included professors, both lay and medical, trained in other institutes. We also were trained in child and adolescent therapy, and exposed to group process. In addition, several of the candidates were from other countries such as Sri Lanka, Greece, Sweden, and Latin American countries which promoted delightful cross-cultural dialogues. Arnold and I flourished in this diverse environment, but Arnold did not feel complete as a psychoanalyst until he was sparked by his reading of Ferenczi which resonated with his adventuresome passionate soul. It is as if Ferenczi ignited an emotional explosion that allowed Arnold's passionate, tender, and generous soul to soar.

After our graduation in 1968 from PGCMH, we maintained a collegial relationship marked primarily by our interest in treating adolescents. Arnold chose what I consider the most difficult psychotherapeutic challenge – adolescent group psychotherapy. Arnold managed to stay in the fray and write a meaningful account of his work with adolescents. I accepted the honor of reviewing his book, *Identity Group Psychotherapy with Adolescents*, which stands as an important stepping stone in the evolution of adolescent group psychotherapy.

My wife and I were very excited about Arnold's invitation to participate in a ten-day trip to Hungary that was aptly termed "Following the Footsteps of Ferenczi." Arnold enlisted the aid of an enterprising travel agent, a couple of Hungarian and/or Ferenczi leaning American psychoanalysts, and a host of psychoanalysts in Hungary. Arnold's team booked us in fine hotels, castles, and villas and arranged for sumptuous lunches and dinners as well as events incorporating the presence of Hungarian analysts as we toured the country. We visited Ferenczi's birthplace, his schools, military station, offices, hospitals, apartment, and finally his grave. We talked with many Hungarian analysts as we toured in a small bus that accommodated about twelve persons. As we explored the country, Arnold and I had many hours together talking of our lives, theories, and practice. I was especially proud to tell Arnold that I had read "The Confusion of Tongues" in 1954; however, I had not realized the significance of the paper.

One incident occurred that showed me an admirable aspect of Arnold's being. Our group of about twenty persons was to have a lunch at a small hotel/restaurant on a hot August Sunday afternoon in a seemingly deserted town. The restaurant was not prepared to feed that large a group as we sat in the restaurant's open hot dining area where we had little or no liquids and no food for an hour or so. Finally, just after we had been served some thin soup and foul-tasting goulash, Arnold and his wife who had disappeared earlier, sauntered into the restaurant, smiling and apparently well-fed. In response to our inquiry, Arnold revealed their impatience, and wandered around the village until they found the only open restaurant – a McDonalds. Thus, I came to respect Arnold's good judgment, his unwillingness to go along with the crowd, and his taking care of himself and his wife. In the same vein, I observed Arnold eventually taking control of the group, mending fences and ensuring that the Hungarians and Americans maintained good relationship. In sum, that ten-day trip remains one of my most cherished professional encounters where I learned so much about Ferenczi and the Hungarian school, the culture, cuisine, and politics of Hungary, and certainly felt closer to Arnold who reflected some of Ferenczi's qualities.

Arnold and I share three other passions – cuisine, jazz, and love of family. Arnold is an excellent chef as exemplified by his exquisite poached salmon. Second, he and I love jazz, particularly the vocalizing and trumpeting of Chet Baker who had been designated as best musician of the year by *Downbeat* magazine. Third, we never tire of talking of our wives, children, and grandchildren. In particular, I relished his openness in discussing very personal experiences as we drove on Friday evenings to teach at the Adelphi Postdoctoral Institute.

One of Arnold's trademarks is his sartorial splendor. While I have been tied to a traditional suit and tie appearance, Arnold has always dressed in a modern and fashionable manner in which he takes great pride. I suppose that Arnold's mode of dress is consistent with his innovativeness and questioning of authority and tradition – the trademarks of Ferenczi.

Another source of my admiration of Arnold is the fact that he had trained and ran in at least two New York City marathons.

I am grateful to Arnold and Henry Kellerman who, during my wife's illness and after her death, encouraged me to meet with them once a month for dinner at various restaurants where we talked of our lives and reminisced about our time at PGCMH. In essence, they helped me grieve the loss of a wife of sixty-five years who they knew.

Professional

Arnold has done more to introduce Ferenczi to American psychoanalysis than any person. His extensive scouring of Ferenczi's writing and his endless scholarly writing about Ferenczi has literally brought Ferenczi back from the dead. His has been a difficult job considering that Freud and Jones had maligned Ferenczi and had banished him from the psychoanalytic world. Arnold has taken the time and made a great effort to contact Hungarian analysts trained and influenced by Ferenczi. Arnold's zeal in buying and placing Elizabeth Severn's papers in the Library of Congress was a monumental step in bringing Ferenczi's work to light. Arnold's multitude of books, papers, and presentations in America and around the world have alerted our profession to the value of "the analyst of last resort."

As an analyst I have asked myself why has there been such a synchrony between Arnold and Sándor. First of all, we must consider Arnold's psychoanalysis. His analyst, Betty Feldman, had been analyzed by Lewis Wolberg, who had been analyzed by Clara Thompson, who had been not only been Ferenczi's analysand, but supervisee and colleague for many years. Knowing Thompson's and Wolberg's work, in which Ferenczi's techniques and theories are discernable, it seems plausible that some of Ferenczi's being had filtered down consciously and unconsciously through the generations. While Arnold can pride himself in being the great, great, grandson of Ferenczi, I see Arnold more as Ferenczi's son, the person to whom Ferenczi might have "passed the psychoanalytic mantle" as Freud intended for Ferenczi. Arnold has Ferenczi's Hungarian soul – it is restless, innovative, romantic, passionate, free-spirited. In addition, Arnold has inherited Ferenczi's articulateness, scholarship, and writing abilities. On the other hand, Arnold has never kowtowed or submitted to authority as Ferenczi had done in respect to Freud. Rather, he has resisted any authoritarianism or personal diminishment, as well illustrated in his struggle with the Dean of Training at PGCMH.

After reading *Elizabeth Severn, The "Evil" Genius* I considered it such an important work that I wrote an extensive book review-essay for the journal, *Modern Psychoanalysis* (Marshall, 2019). Arnold's analysis of Ferenczi's work is brilliant as he clearly describes Ferenczi's hard-earned evolution of theory and technique. Arnold emphasizes the importance of flexibility, empathy, and respect for the analysand's emotional and cognitive contributions. In addition, he underscores the use of a two-person, relational model, the futility of interpretation, and the role of trauma.

My Additional Stake

While I reveal my respect, admiration, and love for Arnold, I must reveal an additional stake I have in Arnold's discovery and resuscitation of Ferenczi. With my last psychoanalyst, I felt an underlying new message in the way my analyst was treating me. As I became more familiar with Ferenczi's writings, I felt my analyst had been influenced by Ferenczi. So, I asked him if he had read Ferenczi. His analytic retort was, "I read everything." After I had studied my analyst's archives, he was not far from that grandiose statement. As I was reading the Freud–Ferenczi correspondence, I noted that Freud had analyzed my analyst's analyst, Lillian Delger Powers, a member of the New York Psychoanalytic Institute. Moreover, it was revealed that Powers had been in analysis/supervision with Ferenczi for six months while he was visiting the United States. When I confronted my analyst with the news, he indicated he had no idea of the Powers–Ferenczi connection, but that his long-term five-day-a-week analysis with her was highly beneficial and somewhat unorthodox. However, I had the answer to my question about the unconventional manner of my analyst. I found additional connections between my analyst and Ferenczi's progeny – several of my analyst's supervisors at the New York

Psychoanalytic Institute were Hungarians who had close contact with Ferenczi. So, I proudly stand with Arnold in having Ferenczi in our psychoanalytic genealogy.

I rejoice in Arnold's ongoing brilliant career. I am thankful that he is bringing the attention of the psychoanalytic world to a psychoanalytic genius. And I am especially grateful to have had the enriching personal and professional association with my Ferenczian cousin.

Reference

Marshall, R.J. *Elizabeth Severn, The 'Evil Genius'.* A Book Review Essay, *Modern Psychoanalysis*, 43: 129–141, 2019.

13 Love and Knowledge

Paul Mattick

Many years ago, when it seemed to me that it might be useful to consult a psychotherapist, a psychoanalyst friend suggested I try Arnold Rachman. Without experience in this matter, I asked her how to deal with a negative reaction on my part – how would I know whether or not I was resistant to the help offered, or just rightfully put off? She told me, "Don't worry about 'resistance.' Just ask yourself, could I love this person? If the answer is No, I'll suggest someone else." As it turned out, the answer to the question, once I had occasion to ask it, was Yes; this led to a long and, for me, fruitful therapeutic association.

That in turn opened the way to a long friendship and even an intellectual collaboration. Many years of individual and group therapy with Arnold aroused a meta-practical interest in his manner of working and its theoretical underpinnings: experience of the possibility of change in feeling and behavior for me (as for many others) raised the question of how this was accomplished. I no longer remember how I began reading Arnold's writing, as an adjunct to understanding the therapeutic work we did together, but I found it fascinating and convincing. The centrality to his thinking of Ferenczi's idea of the "confusion of tongues" dovetailed with my own interest in the role of language-borne categories of experience in the shaping of social reality. Thus I had been thinking about how the classification of certain objects and practices as "art" was essential to their redefinition as matters for aesthetic appreciation rather than other kinds of use. Ferenczi's concept involved an analogous classification as "sexual" feelings and activities that could have quite different functionalities when thought of otherwise.

At the same time, I had been teaching Freud's *Dora* to undergraduates, as part of a class on "modern" ideas. This text, so seductive in its literary quality, presents with especial clarity Freud's combination of brilliance with dogmatic insistence on his understanding of psychic phenomena, despite the absence of validation of his (often bizarre) ideas. It seemed to me that his analysis of Dora was sharply illuminated by the idea of a confusion of tongues, which Arnold had already come to apply to Freud's relationship with his disciple Ferenczi. In imputing Dora of sexual desires for older men – men of his own age – Freud was blindly interpreting Dora's wish for sympathy and affection

DOI: 10.4324/9781003391081-13

in the classically confusing manner of the seducer. This confusion was in fact basic to Freud's thinking, since it powered the idea of "childhood sexuality" according to which, for instance, the infant's enjoyment of the mother's breast is interpreted not (along the most obvious lines) as a matter of enjoyment of both food and affection but as an expression of sexual desire. As Arnold pointed out when we discussed this idea, one could only admire Dora for the strength with which she refused to accept Freud's imputation of a sexual substratum to all her expressions of anxiety and wish for parental affection in the face of abuse at the hands of the adults around her.

When Arnold suggested we write a text together on "the confusion of tongues between Freud and Dora," how could I refuse? Working on a weekly basis with him, discussing ideas, writing, and revising has been one of the great intellectual experiences of my life, not least because of the emotional valences inherent in the topic and avoided by neither of us. It was in the course of our discussions that we came to a reconsideration of the ideas of "resistance" and "transference" central to classical psychoanalysis. In this matter, I was completely convinced by Arnold's insistence on the radically two-person nature of the therapeutic relationship, and so of the therapist's obligation to be aware of this and use it – openly and non-manipulatively – as a means to emotional clarity and freedom. For Freud, Dora's refusal to accept his account of her troubles was a sign of neurotic resistance to the truth. As Arnold saw it, it was praiseworthy resistance to Freud's refusal to listen to her as an equal, to his wish (or need) to impose his reading of their relationship on her. Freud's inability to think about what was at stake in the relationship for him ("countertransference") made it impossible for him to work with her towards an understanding of her situation. What made it possible for me to understand this idea was not just my reading of Ferenczi and my discussions of these questions with Arnold, but my experience of his openness to others in action in both individual and group contexts. It's not, of course, that Arnold did not have, at any moment, his own ideas about what was going on in another person. But he both respected the other's ideas about it and was, therefore, willing to question his own perspective.

For the most part, it seemed to me, Arnold was quite correct in his estimation of psychological situations. But because his goal was not to be right so much as to help, it was possible both to take in his ideas and to find him lovable.

Paul Mattick
New York, August 2020.

14 A Letter to Arnold

Judit Mészáros

Dear Arnold,

Allow me to contribute to this very special issue in this letter with a rather personal tone.

Our relationship probably started in New York in 1991 at the very first internationally attended Ferenczi Conference called "The Legacy of Sándor Ferenczi." I remember I was sitting on a bench with György Hidas when you approached us, sat down and asked how you could help us with our work. A couple of years earlier, in 1988, the year before Hungary's regime change, we had established the Sándor Ferenczi Society. Not long after New York, you and I met again in Budapest at the international conference "The Talking Therapy: Ferenczi and the Psychoanalytic Vocation" in 1993.

Later, we engaged in intensive correspondence during the year I spent as a researcher at the Woodrow Wilson Center (1995–1996), when you were working on your book on Ferenczi, *The Psychotherapist of Tenderness and Passion*, which was published soon afterwards. All this goes back to a time before email, when correspondence meant actual letters often written by hand. Since then, we have met from time to time at Ferenczi conferences in various cities around the world on continents near and far.

You threw yourself into investigating the multiple dimensions of Ferenczi's trauma theory, analyzing the relationship between Ferenczi and Elizabeth Severn, and researching Severn's the so-called "Evil Genius" legacy, which significantly facilitated and contributed a more precise understanding of Ferenczi's work, including an exploration of the motivation and experience of the mutual analysis experiment as well as the Ferenczi legacy as a whole. In those days, Ferenczi was far from part of the mainstream of psychoanalysis. You carried out genuine research, striving to make discoveries through which Ferenczi's new perspectives on psychoanalytic theory and the therapeutic relationship could be reconstructed, and through which the life and work of Severn, a truly contradictory person, also came alive. It was only your passionate devotion that enabled you to keep this work up for decades in addition to your regular daily life. This passion – as far as I can sense it – is part of your life; indeed, it is your lifeblood.

DOI: 10.4324/9781003391081-14

I'd like to return to that conversation on that particular bench in New York. Your question "How can I help?" was sincere, not merely a polite formula. You were there with a generous gift when we had the chance to buy Ferenczi's one-time office in what had once been his villa. During an international fund-raising effort, in the last tense moments right before the purchase deadline in 2011, it was you who provided the significant amount that was still missing. Now, we have seen the International Ferenczi Centre and Archives in operation for ten years. The Ferenczi House Archives today focus on collecting the manuscripts of members of the Budapest School, which by now are referred to as classics of psychoanalysis. Jewish persecution and fascism forced a number of representatives of the school to leave the country. Those difficult times broke the psychoanalytic community that had developed around Ferenczi. Those forced to emigrate, however, contributed richly to the development of modern psychoanalysis in other countries, even as those who remained in Budapest were forced by the Stalinist dictatorship to work underground. While the Ferenczi House Archives collect the legacy of the members of the Ferenczi School who remained in Budapest, they are also enriched by numerous foreign sources. One of the most outstanding collections is your donation of Severn heritage.

When you donated the Severn manuscripts and other materials you had collected to the Library of Congress, you were also mindful of enriching the Archives in Budapest with copies of the original documents. You thus made it possible for this legacy to be available from a European archival source as well as for Severn to return symbolically to Budapest – and back to the Ferenczi House, where some of her analysis took place. Severn knew this milieu very well. It became part of her own psychoanalytic process and the site of her mutual analysis experiment. Now, copies of the manuscripts occupy the same space once visited by Severn and Clara Thompson as well, Ferenczi's well known analysands, where Ferenczi's most important ideas on trauma based on clinical observations were taking shape. The Ferenczi villa was where *Confusion of Tongues* and *Clinical Diary* were written – today his most widely cited studies and the focus of your interest for so many years. Both of these works teach us lessons that had resulted from analysis with Severn.

Your decades of research greatly spurred on the Ferenczi renaissance that began to emerge in the 1980s, and your substantial gifts have made the Ferenczi House possible, a place which represents Ferenczi and the cradle of the Budapest School alike and which is now accessible both to members of our profession and to anyone interested in the history of scholarship and culture.

On the occasion of the International Ferenczi Conference in 2012, which, not surprisingly, was organized around "Faces of Trauma", we had a garden party at Ferenczi House. There, before the professional public, we expressed our gratitude for your magnanimous support in buying this important site.

I am very hopeful that our plan to open the Severn section of the Archives will come to fruition soon with you present. Your offer on that little bench in New York thirty years ago was not only sincere, but greatly impacted the realization of our professional dreams at the time.

Your offer on that little bench in New York came from your heart, and greatly impacted the realization of many of our professional dreams, and your researches greatly contributed to the blossoming of the Ferenczi Renaissance.

For all this, I would like to express my gratitude on behalf of the Ferenczi community in Budapest and to wish you many more beautiful, creative years to come, surrounded by your loving family.

In the hope of seeing you again very soon,

With fondness,
Judit Mészáros

15 Sándor Ferenczi, Robert Fliess, and Me

A Cautionary Tale in Appreciation of Arnold Rachman

Jeffrey Moussaieff Masson

Arnold Rachman is the first (and so far, only one of two) psychoanalysts who have had the courage to say that their profession was wrong, dead wrong, when it came to recognizing the significance of childhood sexual abuse.

Some of you will know that I was a young psychoanalyst in the late 1970s when I became obsessed (the term is legitimate here) with understanding why psychoanalysts refused to believe patients who said they were abused as children. I can vividly remember the first time this came up in one of our seminars. I was a candidate in psychoanalysis at the Toronto Institute of Psychoanalysis. We were ten candidates. I was the only one who was not a medical doctor and a psychiatrist. Our instructor said words to this effect:

> "All of you will already know – except you Masson, the only layperson in this class – that patients come to you and talk about having been sexually abused as a young child. You know that this is not true. What they remember is a fantasy, not a real event. It is what Freud called a 'screen memory' since it screens their own childhood desire. It is, in essence, the Oedipus Complex: they, mostly women, desired their father, but could not admit to this desire. Instead, they imagined that he or some other male had abused them, when in fact this never happened."

I was immediately alarmed; you might even say incensed. "How," I demanded to know, "can you possibly know that something did *not* happen? What evidence do you have for making such an outrageous comment?" The class was appalled by my bad manners. Moreover, they insisted I was simply ignorant. The leader of the seminar explained, patiently, that we did not need evidence, since it was self-evidently a fantasy. All I had to do was open the authoritative *Handbook of American Psychiatry*, and I would see that the incidence of incest was one in a million. As for further authority, Freud himself had first been convinced that women were remembering abuse, but later came to understand that this was not the case. Since I was studying to become a psychoanalyst, surely Freud's own experience was more germane than my own paltry objections?

DOI: 10.4324/9781003391081-15

This comment, and more like it, did little to satisfy me. After all, I reasoned, if someone comes to you and sits on a couch in your living room and tells you with great difficulty that their father (or grandfather or brother or uncle) sexually assaulted them when they were ten years old, your first comment would not be: "No he didn't. You imagined it." But in fact, I was being told that I was naive, uninformed, ignorant, and that in fact, this is exactly what I should think.

I did not believe it for a second and was convinced that I was in an intellectual backwater, and as soon as I was out of Toronto, things would change. Alas, they did not. I managed to score a meeting with Anna Freud while I was still a candidate (this would have been in 1973) and she basically affirmed what I was told in the seminars. "But surely," I asked," is not psychoanalysis the study of personal trauma?" "No," she said, "it is not." The real world was not as important to the psychoanalyst as the world of fantasy. It did not matter *what* happened, only what we *believed* had happened. Whether it did or not was the business of the historian, not the psychoanalyst.

I was disappointed. I eventually went to San Francisco in 1979, by now a fully trained (but renegade) Freudian psychoanalyst. My friends at the time, two senior analysts, Victor Calef and Edward Weinshel, much older than me and far more experienced, and also highly intelligent, told me that, sadly, I was wrong, and everyone else was right.

This is a very long story, and I have tried to tell it in different books (*Final Analysis*, for example) and in other venues. So let me skip to the important part:

For reasons that still remain a mystery to me, Anna Freud eventually took a liking to me and agreed to let me work in her house reading and studying the 169 *unpublished* letters of Freud to Fliess. What I found in these letters was to have a profound influence on my life (it culminated in my losing my license to practice psychoanalysis, being removed from the Freud Archives and from the Freud Copyright, and even losing a three-year lawsuit that went all the way up to the United States Supreme Court – *Masson vs Malcolm and the New Yorker*). But these letters, previously omitted from the edition that Anna Freud first published in German in 1950, and four years later in English, showed that the story of Freud's abandonment of the seduction theory (really the rape of children) was far more complicated and convoluted than we had been led to believe. The letters and other documents I found in Freud's house made it clear: abuse was real and frequent and had a profound influence on the lives of Freud and other analysts, both those who denied the abuse, and, even more importantly, the ONE analyst at the time, who did not: Sándor Ferenczi. I wrote about this in a book published in 1984: *The Assault on Truth: Freud's Abandonment of the Seduction Theory*. I am aware that I could be criticized for my personal views in that book: I agreed that the feminists were right all along: sexual abuse is frequent, it is terrible, and society has always denied it even happens. But what could not be denied is that the letters I found, all unpublished, in Freud's personal desk (who kept them there – and why – a mystery not close to being solved even now, some forty-five or more years later) showed that only Sándor Ferenczi had the courage to tell Freud that he was wrong to give up his belief in the reality of child sexual abuse and that he, Ferenczi, had the clinical experience to prove it to him, (including fascinating sessions with an American patient Elizabeth Severn who was herself trained to work as a psychoanalyst by Ferenczi, and she believed her patients). Ferenczi clearly hoped Freud would take this seriously. He did not. He was alarmed, and he immediately informed his lieutenants to disarm, as it were, the traitor Ferenczi. Ferenczi was so deeply hurt that his hero had abandoned him in such a cruel manner that, I believe, it led to his early death shortly thereafter at the relatively young age of sixty, a lonely and abandoned man (betrayed even by his own analysands, especially the influential Ernest Jones who then betrayed Ferenczi by telling the world that he was paranoid).

It took many years for the psychoanalytic world (mostly, to their credit, in France, thanks to Judith Dupont) to re-evaluate the contribution of Sándor Ferenczi, and I for one believe it is still incomplete. Were you to ask all the world's psychoanalysts what they think of Sándor Ferenczi, I don't believe many would recognize his unique contribution, not so much to psychoanalysis, but to society in general. For his paper, which Freud read in alarm, and which he asked his henchmen (strong word, but in this case, deserved) to disappear it (it was too late to remove the German paper, but the English translation did not until many years later), is, in my opinion, the single best paper *ever* written about the sexual abuse of children: "The Confusion of Tongues between Adults and Children" (in my book I give a new translation from the original German of this remarkable contribution, correcting some errors in the original translation).

But there is one exception, and it is to honor him that I write this essay: Arnold Rachman, a psychoanalyst of some renown, had the courage not only to recognize the importance of Sándor Ferenczi, and to recognize the importance of child sexual abuse, but, and this cannot be overemphasized: he found the papers of Elizabeth Severn; he purchased those papers and he made them available to scholarship, so that now everyone can make up their own mind about this controversy that divided the world of psychoanalysis that is only now receiving its due, in large part thanks to Arnold Rachman.

I have not had the opportunity to meet Arnold Rachman in person, so I am not sure what price he had to pay for his intellectual courage. I am sure it was not cost-free. I say this for the following reason: There is a pattern to be seen here: When Freud first announced, in 1896, to a group of male (not a woman in the room!) psychiatrists that he believed child sexual abuse of both men and women lay behind all forms of neurosis, based on the eighteen cases he had himself analyzed, he was ridiculed to such an extent that he thought of quitting the field. (Anna Freud told me that she left out Freud's response because it made him sound paranoid – he was anything but!) Exactly the same thing happened to his most beloved pupil, Sándor Ferenczi, only this time it was Freud himself who ridiculed Ferenczi, and made sure that all other "right-thinking" analysts did the same and would continue to do so until very recently. Then, when Robert Fliess of all people (for he was the son of Freud's closest friend, Wilhelm Fliess) as a training analyst in New York (much sought after – he analyzed Leonard Shengold and other leading analysts in the ultra-orthodox New York Psychoanalytic Institute) announced that he, like Ferenczi before him, believed in child abuse, and furthermore, as he put it so succinctly and correctly "nobody is made sick from a fantasy, only memories in repression can create neurosis," he was hounded out of the society and forced to move to upstate New York, where he lived in isolation from colleagues until his death in 1975 at a relatively young age. Finally, you now know that the same thing happened to me, only with a better outcome thanks to several strong women in my life.

I had the opportunity recently to speak with Dr. Rachman, now a vigorous and healthy eighty-eight (he swims thirty-three laps every morning, much to my envy!). He told me that in all his training, he was *never* told about Ferenczi at all, let alone about his prescient and precious paper on child abuse (it is filled with extraordinary insights – such as that the abused child must act as a psychiatrist to his own parent). He had to find out about Ferenczi on his own, around 1976, when he found, in the library of the Graduate Center for Mental Health (formerly the Institute for Psychoanalysis) the three-volume English edition of Ferenczi's papers. Nobody had checked them out of the library in the last ten years! Moreover, the silence about Ferenczi (which I speculate was based on the one paper of his that will be read one hundred years from now!), was in spite of the fact that Dr. Rachman's own analyst was the last in a line of analysts going back to Clara Thompson, and Ferenczi himself! How is that for betrayal?

As one of the leading scholars of Ferenczi in the English-speaking world, I am shocked (but not surprised) that Dr. Rachman had rarely been asked to talk about Ferenczi – for even though my own interest in Ferenczi is limited to his one unique essay, it is also true that he was the first to see that patients needed, not just interpretations and even understanding, but also love. He did something daring: mutual analysis, which has not to this day been accepted.

The fact that Dr. Rachman has not had to pay the steep price of being banished for his remarkable courage and his perseverance shows that, to some extent, maybe the world has moved on, even the world of psychoanalysis (though he may be an outlier here). The very fact that this volume in his honor exists is proof that change is afoot, and I am honored to have been asked to recognize and pay homage to this wonderful scholar!

16 A Letter to the Audience about Arnold

Clara Mucci

I met Arnold Rachman at the first Ferenczi Summer School in Florence organized by the Ferenczi Association in July 2017. My seminar (each of the presenters was teaching a one-day seminar) was on "Resilience and how can we counter the end of civilization". Arnold was standing at the back of the room, to my left, with extraordinary attention, and I could see he was seriously taken with a mixture of surprise and a glimpse of enthusiasm. In the end, he raised a few questions, mostly to confirm what I was presenting (as though he wanted to make sure I meant what he had understood), so that he was not mistaken. I was speaking about my "usual things" in my personal battle in psychoanalysis (Mucci, 1998, 2013, 2018): I was stressing, first of all, how Freud disavowed his first trauma theory, based on the "reality" of the "seduction" (a strange word, but very Victorian, to say "abuse" more straightforwardly) in favor of the conflict theory, in 1897, which made the reality of the abuse less the responsibility of the persecutor and more to be blamed on the psyche of the victim. In my view, Freud's renunciation of the seduction theory opened the door to many misunderstandings in what was to be the future of the trauma theory in psychoanalysis. And I wanted to clarify how, on the contrary, it was to Ferenczi and his trauma theory that psychoanalysis in my opinion had to go back in order to regain an ethical position towards trauma and survivors; this going back to Ferenczi would also be the basis for a treatment that held at its stake truth and reparation, distant from what Ferenczi himself, referring to Freud's attitude in treatment, termed openly "hypocrisy." I knew how controversial this point was and still is in psychoanalysis, so I was ready to fight for my point. I had presented these ideas to very traditional psychoanalytic gatherings; renowned psychoanalysts in Italy or elsewhere would listen to me with respect, but unmistakably would restate their point, how the psychic contribution was fundamental in the traumatic consequences, and how a different attitude towards the theory and the practice was not acceptable to psychoanalysis. On the contrary, my position must have surprised Arnold as his position was surprisingly close to mine! And we were both pleasantly surprised, I think. Our comradery was initiated by the fact that we both agreed on an issue that was of fundamental importance to us, humanly and therapeutically, certainly not only for the sake of theory. We were converging on a

DOI: 10.4324/9781003391081-16

version of the trauma theory that was considered highly controversial and that most psychoanalysts did not accept. Not only had Freud disavowed his theory, he had also closed his eyes (or his heart) to the pain of the victims. For us, the bulk of what was necessary for a real reparation of trauma for the survivors coincided with what Ferenczi stressed in his *Clinical Diary* (Ferenczi, raising his voice against Freud: "abreaction is not enough,") and what is fundamental for healing is a totally new and positive relational experience in which not only is truth honored (what really happened for the victim and the perpetrator, with different responsibilities) but the reality of a new experience, a dual and deep relational positive experience, through the benevolent and empathic presence of the therapist, makes possible the retrieval of the denigrated or repressed or dissociated truth of trauma. (I did not know Arnold had written repeatedly on this issue in 1994, 1997, and other works; I had not come across his work at that point. I had been a Literature professor until 2012.)

Very often in fact the reality of trauma (what really happened) is so appalling and unbearable that it is unacceptable to consciousness, so that, in order to survive, some parts of the personality get split, dissociated, or dismembered, and even recalling the event or series of events becomes difficult. This relational and healing or restorative experience for the survivor calls for a different attitude in the therapist, compared to traditional psychoanalysis, taking place on the couch, with only the voice of the analyst; it is more democratic, certainly empathic and deeply involved and committed, what I have further developed in the position of the "embodied witnessing" of the therapist, explaining also neurobiologically and neuroscientifically how this is made possible by the connection of the two minds and bodies in a deep and safe and respectful relationship (Mucci, 2018).

It was on this terrain that we met, and it has remained the common ground of our understanding, commitment, and friendship. I know it strikes a fundamental chord in our being and strengthens our engagement with our work, both intellectually and in practice, in the "emotional" and ethical work of reparation, if I can say so, with the patients. It is more a mission than a job, with strong ethical resonance. I would say it is a vocation in the sense that it raises our consciousness and commitment to a meaning in life that sustains our work and makes our work more meaningful, in a direction that is spiritual or sacred (even though these two words have never entered our relationship or writings, so far).

On this terrain, real intellectual passion and involvement, and personal engagement were reinforced by our agreement on further points: the reality of trauma and the importance (and the devastating consequences) of abuse in shaping the life of the subject and therefore the crucial impact of what interpersonal trauma creates leads to what Rachman has in his many writings clarified and renamed as "Trauma Disorder" and "Trauma Analysis (Rachman, 2018 but starting as early as 1988), notions that I would situate within what generally goes under the rubric of Complex PTSD, relational and intersubjective, still not recognized by DSM-5. I would further situate this kind of trauma disorder due to interpersonal trauma and abuse in the second level of what I have discussed in my description of the three levels of the trauma of human agency, to be distinguished by trauma due to natural catastrophes or devoid of evil intention (Mucci, 2018).

In other words, this initial intellectual agreement on trauma stretches far beyond the theoretical assumptions behind it and it is in fact the crux of our engagement to a certain kind of therapeutic commitment. Re-establishing the will and listening to the voice of the victim resituates in my opinion within psychoanalysis a place of truth and commitment where theory per se is not the most important thing if it does not involve a different practice in the interest of regaining the truth and the strength of the survivor.

We both find in Ferenczi the starting point of this different psychoanalytic view or commitment, which stretches beyond a relational view of psychoanalysis, in my opinion, to include a two-person psychology, extending the Freudian intrapsychic perspective of the subject, into a dual unconscious, in continual communication since birth, or in fact even before then, *in utero*. It also reclaims on original position towards the truth for the subject who has undergone trauma in the sense of abuse. This leads to a redefinition, in my opinion, of psychoanalysis as a practice of testimony or witnessing the trauma of the victim; "embodied" in the sense that it takes the body and the mind of the survivor (the brain is the body) and at the same time the body and mind of the therapist for the healing to come through. In this view, the interpretation being only or mostly cognitive is not the main tool for healing, if it is not accompanied by empathy and relieving of the emotional truth of the traumatic scene/s with an actual experience of reparation, a new relational experience for the mind and body. Following attachment theory, I would say that disorganization or insecurity of attachment, created by interpersonal trauma, needs to be worked through to establish secure attachment, and that can be done only in a relationship. As Rachman phrases it in *Ferenczi's Confusion of Tongues Theory of Trauma: A Relational Neurobiological Perspective*, which we are presently working on, "what has been damaged by a relationship needs to be repaired in a relationship" (Rachman and Mucci, 2024).

So, this kind of recognition was very important and foundational for us. But becoming involved with the books' writings together did not start immediately. In the meantime, we had traded our books (he sent many of his books to me, and I gave him what I had in English on trauma). I had read his fundamental book on incest written in 2015 with Susan A. Klett (Rachman and Klett, 2015) and his edited work on the Budapest School of psychoanalysis (Rachman, Ed., 2016), which was a building block for the recognition of the new development of psychoanalytic theory started by Ferenczi. Again, the cogency of his points struck me as so close to my work on empathy that I was developing through the interdisciplinary connection of attachment, neuroscience, and psychoanalysis: what Arnold called the "empathic" connection was strikingly close to my view of the emotional participation of the analyst for the true healing to take place; the restoration of a place of truth that from an individual basis became in my opinion a social and collective way of reconnecting to some levels of justice. I have defined this place of truth and relationality in individuals and society as "connectedness" (Mucci, 2013). I believe that when Arnold and I refer to a "two-person psychology" which is instrumental for individual growth and well-being, we also include a possibility for a "we" to be created as a result of that safe "me and you" position. This is the foundation of restoration that even individual therapy brings forth in society. I see this point is also clarified by Judith Herman in her wonderful book *Trauma and Recovery*.

There was another occasion in which our work crossed (before our present collaboration I mean), and that was his invitation to me to contribute to an issue within *Psychoanalytic Inquiry* about how several professionals had arrived at the practice of psychoanalysis from different detours. I had been a professor of English Literature specializing in Shakespeare's plays and writing books on a psychoanalytic understanding of those texts before retraining in clinical psychology and entering an institute of psychoanalytic psychotherapy. So Arnold invited me to contribute, and it was also the occasion for a profound revelation for me. I don't know exactly why, but it was for me a sort of coming out, (of what the detours of my life had been for me and where they had taken me) – a disclosure that I was making in front of an audience of gifted and renowned colleagues. It was very powerful for me and unexpected. I owe to Arnold this "passage" into a psychological unveiling of myself that I think led finally to the possibility of my publishing my personal poems; written long before in those troublesome years that required years of psychotherapy (not only to become an analyst but before, when I was for many years a patient, teaching with a strong passion for psychoanalytic theory and texts).

Another Congress in Florence on Ferenczi was another joyful and intense occasion to communicate; this time Arnold had just published his revolutionary work on Elizabeth Severn, and he was presenting a paper based on how mainstream psychoanalysis had removed her legacy and her work through *Todschweigen* (death by silence) (Rachman, 2018). It was 2018. More conversations and more time together led to the development of projects of writing together on trauma to discuss in depth our point of view on the psychoanalysis of trauma. During my summers in New York, when I could take time off from my Italian university, our discussions would start in his office, commenting on our papers or other work, surrounded by the most beautiful Manhattan views. The same discussions also led me to give a lecture on Ferenczi and trauma theory for the Post-Graduate Psychoanalytic Institute, under Arnold's supervision, in 2018.

Then Covid hit when there was the planned celebration of all the contributors for the coming out of the book on the *Different Paths Towards Becoming a Psychoanalyst and Psychotherapist: Personal Passions, Subjective Experiences and Unusual Journeys* (Rachman and Kooden, 2021). I think it was after this planned "reunion" during the deprivation of Covid times (I had not been able to go back to New York for over two years) that Arnold and I decided to start a routine of meeting online during the weekend (Saturday mostly) to give the latest update on our work and ideas.

Arnold was intensively writing his remarkable last volume on *Psychoanalysis and Society's Neglect of the Sexual Abuse of Children, Youth, and Adults* (Rachman, 2022). He had already in mind most of the chapters, and I added for *Confusion of Tongues* the part that is my expertise – the difference between the trauma of human agency compared to trauma due to natural catastrophes. This difference is where the confusion of tongues, in my opinion, becomes a most important and unfortunately common problem in children's upbringing in all places at all times and social classes, incest being the most disturbing and less recognized, therefore even most difficult to accept and work through by the survivors. We would also meet online on Zoom, from Milan to New York, to focus on our own chapters and to kindle the fire of our work. Sometimes I would think I was too tired, or we did not have urgent business to solve from the previous weeks, but unmistakably the meeting would take something from the ashes and revitalize some dull or dormant element. Even though these were late after-dinner meetings for me I would always be ener-gized and more active than at the beginning of them. I guess that is also not only the power of the intellectual mind that Arnold obviously has, but the caliber of the analyst, making real things unknown or apparently not openly resonant, and revitalizing parts that are dormant or disconnected. It is also his creativity that is always capable of recognizing where the originality and the strength of some ideas or views lie, and that works relentlessly, like yeast, bringing forth full potential. We would unmistakably have more ideas and more projects about plans and work to do at the end of the meetings than at the beginning. For instance, now as we are finishing the *Confusion of Tongues* book (Rachman and Mucci, 2022), a next book is appearing in our minds (always in Arnold's mind first then taking shape also in my mind with other details and different features as we join our views together), about the present relevance of the Oedipus Complex and even about its origin. Notoriously, Ferenczi in the *Clinical Diary* (1988) and in his paper on "The Confusion of Tongues" (1980) criticized the Oedipus Complex as a fantasy of Freud, not a necessity for the human psyche. In the "Confusion of Tongues" paper, more-over, the Oedipus Complex is seen as a necessity of the passionate view of the adult towards the children, while the latter just need tenderness. And we are going to present a series of lectures on trauma for the Post-Graduate Institute in New York, which outline what we are presently shaping. For the same insti-tute, we have proposed a course on trauma that is going to be taught in part by Arnold and in part by me, in the spring; and we will focus on the coming out book (On confusion of tongues as a political paradigm not only in Ferenczi or in psychoanalysis).

In other words, the truth of what comes out in our meetings is immediately turned into another project, another idea, another chapter, something that is important to share with others. The clarity and depth of his thoughts as we debate or discuss something are astonishing. His piercing knowledge and awareness come out with simple clarity and apparent effortlessness. This simple and strongly aware attitude has helped me bring forth my ideas with more courage and sharpness. It is difficult to express the sense of empowerment that our work together gives me. I think the extension of Arnold's attitude of sincere interest and empathic ethical and rigorous involvement brings to the other person the courage and freedom to take things out.

Finally, another major involvement for us, though less expressed openly in our talks, is my deep commitment to the Holocaust and the trauma of the Jews during the Second World War. One summer we paid a wonderful visit to the Museum of Jewish Heritage in New York, where besides an atrocious documentary of the actual capture and trial of Adolf Eichmann we had the most delicious Jewish food at the Deli in the building. This tradition of having bagels with lox, soup, and other delicious Jewish meals has always been honored by us even though I don't belong literally to the Jewish heritage (but at heart, everybody says I belong to the "tribe" – a reference from *The Merchant of Venice* of course!).

This is almost all about our work together and how I began to work with Arnold, and how I hope we continue, with other projects. If I were to summarize his major and strongest points, at the cost of reducing a great bulk of his work and ideas, I would still recapitulate it in this way, also following his outstanding bibliography:

1 Psychoanalysis is a dual relational enterprise that can mend the world ("Tikkun Olam") starting from two people meeting regularly within the safety of the psychoanalytic rules.
2 Confusion of tongues as a power structure in society not only between relatives or different sexes but as a dangerous structure with many connections.
3 Identification with the aggressor as an internalized part is always in danger of being repeated in individuals and society.
4 The necessity of a talking cure that is neither a power relationship nor an intellectual showing off of knowledge, but a caring attitude involving empathy and (why not use this word that Ferenczi had the courage to use) – LOVE.

References

Ferenczi, S. The confusion of tongues between adults and children: The language of tenderness and passion. In M. Balint (Ed.), *Final Contributions to the Problems and Methods of Psychoanalysis*, Vol. VIII, pp. 156–157. New York: Bruner/Mazer (original work published in 1949, written in 1933), 1980.
Ferenczi, S. *The Clinical Diary of Sándor Ferenczi*, Ed. J. Dupont, Trans. M. Balint and N.Z. Jackson. Cambridge, MA: Harvard University Press, 1988.
Mucci, C. *Il dolore estremo. Il trauma da Freud alla Shoah*. Roma: Borla, 1998.

Mucci, C. *Beyond Individual and Collective Trauma: Intergenerational Transmission, Psychoanalytic Treatment and the Dynamics of Forgiveness.* London: Karnac (reprinted, Routledge), 2013.

Mucci, C. *Borderline Bodies: Affect Regulation Therapy for Personality Disorders.* New York: Karnac, 2018.

Rachman, A. *Elizabeth Severn. The "Evil Genius" of Psychoanalysis.* New York: Routledge, 2018.

Rachman, A. The confusion of tongues theory: Ferenczi's legacy in psychoanalysis. In A. Haynal and E. Falzeder (Eds.), *100 Years of Psychoanalysis,* pp. 235–255. London: Karnac, 1994.

Rachman, A. *Sándor Ferenczi: The Psychotherapist of Tenderness and Passion.* Northvale, NJ: Jason Aronson, 1997.

Rachman, A., Ed. *The Budapest School of Psychoanalysis: The Origin of a Two-Person Psychology and Empathic Perspective.* London: Routledge, 2016.

Rachman, A. *Psychoanalysis and Society's Neglect of the Sexual Abuse of Children, Youth, and Adults. Redressing Freud's Original Theory of Sexual Abuse and Trauma.* New York: Routledge, 2022.

Rachman, A. The Relationship between Freud and Ferenczi: The Meaning for the Development of Psychoanalysis. Presentation *Postgraduate psychoanalytic Institute for Mental Health.* New York City, March, 1988.

Rachman, A. and Klett, S. *Analysis of the Incest Trauma: Retrieval, Recovery, Renewal.* London: Karnac, 2015.

Rachman, A. and Kooden, H., Eds. *Different Paths towards Becoming a Psychoanalyst and Psychotherapist: Personal Passions, Subjective Experiences and Unusual Journey.* London: Routledge, 2021.

Rachman, A. and Mucci, C. *Ferenczi's Confusion of Tongues Theory of Trauma: A Relational Neurobiological Perspective.* New York: Routledge, 2024.

17 Kaddish for Arnold and Reneszánsz for Ferenczi

Salvador Rocha Pineda

Last year at Marienbad[1]

"The Marienbad Elegy" is a very personal poem by Goethe. He wrote it between September 5 and 12, 1823 in a carriage on the road from Karlsbad to Weimar.

> *I have already lost the Universe and I have lost myself*
> *myself – I, beloved of the gods –.*
> *their Pandora's Box have poured me,*
> *rich in atrocious gajes or horoscopes.*
> *They tempt me with the prodigal waterfall*
> *of the joys ... and they sink me into nothingness.*

While Freud was on vacation in the same spa where Goethe wrote his Elegy, in Karlsbad[2] July 1912, Ernest Jones and Sándor Ferenczi were concerned about Adler's publication, a year earlier in the Vienna Psychoanalytic Association, of an article that went against some fundamental concepts of psychoanalysis, which proposed strategies in favor of a psychology of the individual consciousness, in order to improve the quality of life and happiness of the person – very similar to the current intersubjective theories in vogue.

They were also disturbed by William Stekel's modification of the term perversion to paraphilia; by Jung's work, which ignored infantile sexuality and hardly quoted Freud in his publications.

Jones and Ferenczi agreed to form a secret committee with the purpose of preserving the fundamental principles of psychoanalysis. Ernest Jones emphasized mainly the existence of the unconscious psyche, the concept of repression, and the importance of infantile sexuality. Jones invited Rank to join and they communicated to Freud. On August 1, 1912, Freud was enthusiastic about the idea and added Hans Sachs and Karl Abraham as well as Ferenczi's friend, the philosopher Anton von Freund, to the project.

As a sign of thanks and camaraderie, Freud gave some Greek cameos from his private collection of antiquities, later they would all be set in gold rings.

DOI: 10.4324/9781003391081-17

Freud would wear a Greco-Roman cameo with the head of Zeus-Jupiter, until he offered it to Max Eitingon when he recruited him for the committee.

It is in these disturbing moments that Freud published, in 1913, "Totem and Taboo"; a work where he develops his ideas on "parricide." It is impossible not to think of some relationship between the essay and the problems of fidelity among colleagues.

Welshman Ernest Jones was appointed chairman of this secret committee, which was to bear the nickname of "The Ring." The last meeting of the Committee, in which all its members were present, took place in the last week of August 1923. They met in San Cristoforo, near Lake Caldonazzo, in the Dolomites; the Committee fulfilled its purposes for some time.

Wiesbaden, 1932 Ferenczi

Before the XIIth International Psychoanalytic Congress, which took place from September 4 to 7, 1932, in Wiesbaden, Ferenczi traveled to meet Freud and present his paper, which would eventually be entitled: *Confusion of Languages between Adults and the Child*. According to Ingeborg Meyer-Palmedo's notes, the beginning of the congress was set for September 4, but the "first scientific session" started from "Saturday, September 3 at 9 p.m." with Ferenczi's paper. This choice to present before the start of the congress could have resulted from the differences of opinion between Jones, Eitingon, Brill, and Ophuijsen on the issue of whether Ferenczi's paper could be completely blocked.

On September 2 Freud and Ferenczi met for the last time. The meeting went badly. The atmosphere was explosive from the beginning. A letter from Freud to Anna the next day testifies to Freud's version of the meeting and tells of the painful estrangement of the two men.

Freud rejected the paper and urged Ferenczi to renounce his presentation and to refrain from publishing it for a certain period of time, in the hope that he would rectify it.

Prof- Dr. Freud
Vienna, IX. Berggasse 19, 3/9/1932

My dear Anna

The Ferenczi's came (…) She was loving as always, he conveyed an enormous coldness. The first thing he said, without a question or a greeting, was: I want to read you my lecture. He read it and what I heard shook me. He has made a total regression to the etiological conceptions in which I believed and published 35 years ago, that the usual causes of neuroses are serious childhood sexual traumas, he said almost verbatim the same as I did then.(…) The conclusions were totally confused, clearly forced. All so silly, or at least it seems so, because it is so dishonest and incomplete. Now you will have listened to the lecture and have your own opinion. In the middle of the lecture came Brill (...) he said to me under his breath, he is not sincere. The same as with Rank, but much sadder. Have the best time you can in Wiesbaden and don't take anything that happens too badly or too seriously.

Love
Dad.

Let us recall that the first divergences between Freud and Ferenczi did not apparently concern, at first, more than technical problems, but had visibly extended since May 1929 to theoretical aspects.

The two great analysts never met again. Ferenczi died on May 22, 1933. He was suffering from pernicious anemia, which Freud learned of in early October 1932.

As the notes to the edition inform us, Anna was in Wiesbaden on the occasion of the above-mentioned congress. A. Brill, the New York psychoanalyst alluded to in the letter, had visited Freud on August 23 and 24 and had then gone to Budapest with Radó; after his return, they had informed Freud, on August 28, of Ferenczi's condition and his new ways.

Arnold

My friend Uriel García Varela,[3] who had been very interested in the study of Ferenczi for some years and had naturally approached the International Sándor Ferenczi Network, invited me to what would be the last seminar of his teacher Arnold Rachman.[4]

I must say that it was a privilege to have attended the seminar. To meet Rachman, always enthusiastic, generous, and open to new ideas. The discussion about the silencing of Ferenczi's work, what Rachman calls *Todschweigen* – death through silence – was part of the discussions.

On a personal note, during my formative years I became acquainted with J.M. Masson's book *The Assault on Truth; Freud Suppression of the Seduction Theory*, published through the generosity of K.R. Eissler, Anna Freud, and Muriel Gardiner, who facilitated research and access to the archives.

It was for me a revelation and a stimulus, and a surprise, the silence, both of my teachers, as well as in the IPA: *Todschweigen*. Ferenczi undoubtedly loved psychoanalysis and questioned, as it should be, the master. Freud's fears that he would deviate from the roots now seem to us exaggerated.

We can say, following Heidegger's ideas, that he dared to truly think psychoanalysis.

As Rank and Ferenczi said it is not enough to know what the patient is feeling, but we have to expire it for ourselves because, obviously, it is not the same to be in prison than to read what it means to be in prison.[5]

Thinking about it from the inside, not in an aseptic theoretical way, several times, Rachman pointed out that Ferenczi had three analyses: with Freud, the master, with the "soul finder" Groddeck, and with the "evil genius" Elizabeth Severn. If that doesn't change your life, then I don't know what could.

Groddeck says,[6] "The soul is infected by the body, and the body by the contents of the soul; in reality one cannot speak of a self, because one does not live, but is lived by an it."

Another important teaching of Rachman's seminar was the possibility of thinking about Kohut's work, which is so enthusiastic about empathy and which makes no mention of Ferenczi, nor of the concept of mutuality. However, he seems to profit from it.

The works of Kohut (1959), "Introspection, Empathy, and Psychoanalysis" (1959), or *The Analysis of the Self: A Systematic Approach to the Psychoanalytic Treatment of Narcissistic Personality Disorders* (1971), much later than Ferenczi, overlook all the Hungarian's contribution, which in different ways had already been exposed by Michael Balint, Karen Horney herself, etc. – an eagerness for originality and complacent ignorance on the other side.

Arnold was a unique guy, fully identified with Ferenczi, in his part rebellious, yet affable, capable of questioning what others accepted as doctrinaire. I have no words of thanks for the opportunity to have had the experience of a critical seminar, with a psychoanalyst of such stature, not at all complacent and always in search of new horizons.

Tzaddik in Hebrew means someone just, righteous. A man who complies with the moral principles of Judaism; also a charismatic leader of the Hasidic community, treated with the utmost respect by his followers who believe he has the power to perform miracles – Arnold was a good *Tzaddik* to the fullest extent of the word.

I came in during the Kaddish who was a jazz and *Yankee* enthusiast; as a good New Yorker, then, I dedicate and recommend to readers a beautiful piece by Karen Mantler, daughter of my admired Carla Bley and Michael Mantler: My cat Arnold.

Notes

1 *L'Année dernière à Marienbad* is a 1961 film by Alain Resnais full of nods to psychoanalytic language. Written by Alain Robbe-Grillet and inspired by the *Invention of Morel* by Bioy Casares.

2 In a valley surrounded by mountains *Karlovy Vary (Karlsbad* in German) is one of the spas of Bohemia as *Františkovy Lázně, Teplice and Mariánské Lázně*, in German: *Marienbad* (Maria's Baths) famous spa of the Region of Karlovy Vary, Czech Republic, 170 km west of Prague. Seat of thermal baths is a city mentioned since the XII century, it acquired reputation during the Austro-Hungarian Empire, where people like Johann Wolfgang von Goethe, Frédéric Chopin, Anton Bruckner, Franz Kafka, Henrik Ibsen, Mark Twain, Richard Wagner, Stefan Zweig, Sigmund Freud, Alfred Nobel, Gustav Mahler, and Friedrich Nietzsche, besides kings, czars, princes, and members of the European nobility went to rest and to cure

themselves. It reached its splendor between 1870 and 1914, with another important period between the two world wars.

3 Uriel García Varela, recently translated for *Cuadernos de Psicoanálisis* (July–December 2023) vol. LVI, no. 3, 4, a paper by Christopher Fortune: "The influence of Georg Groddeck's friendship on Sándor Ferenczi," and published in *Revista de Psicoanálisis de Madrid*, 39(100) (February 2024), "Freud, Ferenczi y el orden materno."

4 Arnold W. Rachman, PhD, FAGPA Training and Supervising Analyst at the Institute of the Postgraduate Psychoanalytic Society, New York; Clinical Professor of Psychology at Derner Institute, Adelphi University; Associate Professor of Psychiatry, New York University Medical School; on the Faculty of the Trauma and Disaster Studies Program, New York University Postdoctoral Program in Psychoanalysis; on the Board of Directors, Sándor Ferenczi Study Center, New School for Social Research; and author of: *Sándor Ferenczi: The Psychotherapist of Tenderness and Passion* and *Psychotherapy of Difficult Cases: Flexibility & Responsiveness in Clinical Practice*.

5 Horney, K., *El Proceso Terapéutico*, p. 277. Madrid: Ediciones La Llave, 2003.

6 Groddeck G., *El Buscador de almas*, p. 411. Mexico: Sexto Piso, 2014.

References

Freud, S. *Totem and Taboo: Some Points of Agreement between Lives of Savages and Neurotics*. Wien: Hugo Heller, 1913.

Kohut, H. Introspection, empathy, and psychoanalysis: An examination of the relationship between mode of observation and theory, *Journal of the American Psychoanalytic Association*, 7: 459–483, 1959.

Kohut, H. *The Analysis of the Self: A Systematic Approach to the Psychoanalytic Treatment of Narcissistic Personality Disorders*. New York: International Universities Press, 1971.

Masson, J. M. (1984). *The assault on truth: Freud's suppression of The Seduction Theory*. New York: Farrar, Strauss, & Giroux.

Rachman, A. *Psychoanalysis and Society's Neglect of the Sexual Abuse of Children, Youth, and Adults. Redressing Freud's Original Theory of Sexual Abuse and Trauma*. New York: Routledge, 2022.

18 Arnold Rachman

Reminiscences from Bronx to Budapest

Robert Prince

I first met Arnold when I was a graduate student in clinical psychology and have known him across many different contexts since 1972 – as an analyst, teacher, supervisor, collaborator, and friend. These many years give me not only the privileged personal vantage these roles confer but also the opportunity to experience his interactions with many other people. The word that best captures Arnold's essence is passion, the same word he used in the title of his Ferenczi book (Rachman, 1997) and the trait that he brought to his interactions and which he brings to everything that he does, whether athletic (he's a marathon runner), artistic (he has experimented with multiple forms), or psychoanalytic. His passion stands out and inspires.

When we met, he was passionate about Erik Erikson who informed his work identity and work with adolescents. Erikson, when I met him, was his pole star and adolescents were a population that were a natural fit for Arnold's energy and personality. They required active engagement, authenticity, empathy mixed with the necessary dollops of firmness, and did not allow room for insincerity. The adolescent group was his forte, it always challenged him and he had more than his share of "difficult" and "acting act" youngsters who were engaged by his unique personal qualities. In his first book, *Identity Group Psychotherapy with Adolescents* (Rachman, 1975), he was already exploring the uses of the analysts' self as the loft to enable the therapy to soar, and proposed the all-important role of providing his confused and struggling patients with an object for identification.

In this context, I was engaged by Arnold but knew I was too different to be exactly like him and our relationship would unfold according to movement toward identifications in the context of radical differences. A very small vignette that illustrates his profound influence dates to our first getting to know each other. He had started as a therapy supervisor in my doctoral program in clinical psychology and had offered, or I had asked who remembers, to listen to an audiotape of a research interview with a young adult child of concentration survivors. I was trying to elicit psycho-historical themes in her life for my doctoral dissertation. I was frustrated and critical of her because the material seemed to me to be flat, did not seem to advance my project and I was hoping he could hear something in the interview that I could not. I was

DOI: 10.4324/9781003391081-18

looking for something of deep dynamic significance. My thought was my inexperience and lack of knowledge occluded insight into some pertinent unconscious associations that would be obvious to a seasoned analyst. I thought I knew the direction in which the answers could be found – it never crossed my mind I was on the wrong road.

Arnold's reaction to my summary of her life story and hearing her response to my questions on the tape was totally unexpected and has stayed with me, serving me as a person and clinician, for almost fifty years. I had been feeling critical and dismissive, regarded her responses as superficial and concrete, not of psychoanalytic grade. Arnold reacted to her warmly; he liked her and thought she was a lovely person. Very small concepts and simple words for a huge epiphany.

To unpack this, Arnold always had an uncanny ability to recognize the positive. Talking to him about a patient, he identified a core of, call it a value, health, strength, or virtue, the appreciation of which led somewhere worthwhile. Of course, the same was true about talking to him about myself. What I learned from Arnold was, above all, that an attitude of friendliness and generosity is not only compatible with both being human and being a psychoanalyst but may be a precondition for it. Over the years Arnold referred me patients, some he had seen but for some reason or other couldn't continue with, or others he had consultations with. They were rarely what I thought of as "good" analytic patients but somehow ended up coming to me with a kind of enthusiasm for psychoanalysis as he introduced it to them. I always appreciated the positive experience they took away from their meeting with him. It was more of a challenge to find in myself the sensitivity to reproduce it.

That friendliness, warm acceptance made the work possible. Which is not to imply Arnold was nothing but ubiquitously supportive. On the contrary, from this position of friendliness, he was even more able to be confrontational, to experiment, and take risks in the form of creative therapeutic strategies and experiments, all of which were enabled by his essential generosity. He knew how to keep even forceful confrontation from being diminishing to a person's sense of worth but enabling their growth. It is not surprising that was he drawn to and developed expertise in group therapy as a complement to individual work. The group was a natural venue for his enthusiasm and energy as well as his early willingness to allow himself to be examined and engage. Judicious self-disclosure became very much part of his process. It was the seed of the meaningfulness he later found in mutual analysis and the contributions of Elizabeth Severn.

Arnold had no small measure of the rebellious in his spirit, not unlikely brought from the part of the Bronx he came from, a few levels grittier than the gritty section I came from, which fostered an assertiveness which when translated into an institutional context did not allow for submission to orthodoxies and passive submission to received wisdom. He certainly read the book but did not worship it and that could create friction with institutionalized authority. In his early work Arnold espoused and displayed a commitment to a humanistic psychology that emphasized a positive view of the person in contrast to a hermeneutic of suspicion. The latter is as inherently critical as the former offers possibilities for growth and self-actualization that were emphasized and supported through all possible means while not artificially limited by rules imposed by authoritarian structures. Erikson's deeply developmental perspective led to a view that psychotherapy helped people discover and build who they were and fosters a humanistic role model that was resonant for him. He wrote, the therapist functions as an "identity role model who is an emotionally engaged positive role model" (Rachman, 1975, p. 7). His personal background, growing up in a "tough" section of the Bronx, fostered orientation to including psychosocial influences and real experiences.

The flexibility, inventiveness, tapping into reserves of creativity, spontaneity, exploration of boundaries, tolerance, and acceptance required for success with adolescents in Arnold's early work, and particularly the necessity of rising to meet the challenges they posed, prepared him for his discovery of Sándor Ferenczi in whom he found a kindred spirit.

Arnold discovered Ferenczi shortly after *Identity Group Psychotherapy* was published. He came across a reference in the context of researching the "active techniques" he had found necessary in working with adolescents. He had no great expectations since Ferenczi's work had not been part of his curriculum, and he describes a rush of excitement as he began reading the Hogarth Press three volume collection (Ferenczi, 1950, 1952, and 1955). He writes, "at last, I was reading a psychoanalyst with whom I could identify" (Rachman, 1997, p. xiii), that he found in Ferenczi's writing a path to deep self-exploration and personal growth. Looking back, he writes,

> I have had a long and difficult intellectual, emotional, and interpersonal struggle in becoming a psychoanalyst. For the first fourteen years of my analytic career, I did not have an exemplar in psychoanalysis with whom to identity until I discovered Sándor Ferenczi.
> (Rachman, 2014, p. 182)

His discovery of Ferenczi's ideas was accompanied by another serendipitous discovery, only possible, in those days before the ubiquity of digital records. In looking at the cards pasted in the Ferenczi volumes, he found that those volumes had only been taken out twice in the preceding thirty years. Arnold began to trace the historical arc of Ferenczi's role in psychoanalysis and set himself the mission of reviving Ferenczi's essential contributions, restoring to psychoanalysis a vital body of thought the loss of which had created a vacuum. He saw the analytic community had introduced the practice of *Todschweigen*, Death by Silence (Rachman, 1999). Arnold was never one who submitted to being silenced and he felt a personal obligation to rescue Ferenczi from the injustices that had been done to him and contribute to a Ferenczi renaissance. It is my belief that Arnold never, despite his prolific writing and lectures, to say nothing of his original contributions to Ferenczi scholarship, received the degree of recognition he deserved for his role in the reintroduction of Ferenczi's work into the psychoanalytic mainstream. This perhaps is the fate of first discoverers and perhaps has something to do with his own complex stance toward organized psychoanalysis and determination to set his own course.

I knew Arnold during this period of initial discovery. I think he continued as basically himself but the validation he found reading Ferenczi resulted in him being more so. I'm not even sure that what he experienced as a "discovery" was as much of a discovery as it was a recognition of what was already present in him, and his Ferenczi scholarship was something that sharpened his articulation of his humanistic instincts.

Probably what changed more was a kindling of his reaction to the constraints of mainstream orthodoxies and hierarchies. He did develop a determination "To right a wrong of history of psychoanalysis" (Rachman, 1997, p. xvi) and injustice to Ferenczi from the psychoanalytic establishment. His historical researches would lead him to conclude that a conspiracy originating in Ferenczi's refusal to accept the presidency of the International Psychoanalytic Association (IPA) and the initial reading of the Confusion of Tongues paper to Freud and then at the Wiesbaden Conference in 1932 – a conspiracy to suppress Ferenczi's work.

This thread of fighting injustice runs through Arnold's work. On many levels it is captured in Arnold's exploration of the "Confusion of Tongues" (Ferenczi, 1933) concept and the drama of Ferenczi's insistence on reading the paper to Freud before the Wiesbaden Conference and the subsequent slanders involving Ferenczi's mental health.

Arnold reasoned that the reaction to Confusion of Tongues, particularly Ferenczi's denunciation, one that alienated him from his colleagues, was due to professional hypocrisy which interfered with the exposure of the dark secrets in middle-class families. Second in importance only to Ferenczi's contributions to the technique of psychoanalysis was his theory of trauma and return to early Freud's focus on the actual harm done to the person and the sexual exploitation of children. Arnold picked up Ferenczi's banner.

In a volume titled *The Budapest School of Psychoanalysis* (Rachman, 2016a), he christens a Budapest School composed of a Hungarian group de facto formed by Ferenczi. In doing so, he helps to, in his words, "establish the reality of the Budapest school's influence on the evolution of psychoanalysis" (p. 209). He posits "there has arisen out of the work of the pioneering Hungarian analysts who were influenced by Sándor Ferenczi a distinct and significant perspective that has evolved as an alternative to the Freudian tradition" (pp. 209–210).

In his own contribution, "Psychoanalysis' Neglect of the Incest Trauma: The Confusion of Tongues between Psychoanalysis and Society," Rachman (2016b) summarizes and expands some of his previous contributions elucidating the controversy over Freud's change in focus from actual seduction of children to children's sexual fantasies, that is, the formulation of the Oedipus complex. He writes, "The legacy of the Budapest school is to contrast the Oedipal view with Ferenczi's Confusion of Tongues theory, which restored the focus on the adult abuser" (p. 155). He proceeds to detail the Confusion of Tongues paradigm, connecting it to neglect of the incest trauma and makes a plea for addressing incest trauma and sexual abuse in society and psychoanalysis. He expresses the view it has opened up an understanding of how important the issue of trauma has been in understanding psychological disorders and personality development – an issue he believes psychoanalysis and society have neglected.

Arnold's commitment to treatment of the incest trauma deepened with his exploration of the contribution of Elizabeth Severn. His discovery of Severn in many ways paralleled his discovery of Ferenczi, bringing her from obscurity to centrality. As he investigated their observations and reactions to each other in their mutual analysis, he found that together they were laying the basis for changing the analytic encounter by co-creating a set of non-interpretative measures, such as, clinical empathy, analyst self-disclosure, countertransference analysis, to say nothing of mutual analysis itself, to develop a new kind of analysis to treat psychological suffering and illness, which had its origin in actual experience. He writes,

> It is my belief that Severn was an unsung hero of psychoanalysis because she used her illness to push herself to recovery, helping pioneer an evolutionary treatment for the incest trauma and contribute to the Confusion of Tongues theory of trauma.
>
> (Rachman, 2010, p. 149)

He continues to laud her,

> She used her intellect, assertiveness, knowledge of therapy and her illness to relentlessly explore the darkest recesses of her own mind, while pushing her analyst to do the same. Her analyst, for the first time in analytic history developed an "invitro" experiment in the use of subjectivity to analyze an individual suffering from trauma.
>
> (Rachman, 2014a, p. 149)

Arnold's creativity extends beyond psychoanalysis. For a period of time he experimented with collages and for my fiftieth birthday gave me one which he had created from photographs surreptitiously obtained from various moments in my life. In writing this set of impressions, I can visualize a collage of points in space and time from his life. Perhaps part of our connection comes from the fact that our geographical maps overlap. I also come from the Bronx, from parents of Hungarian origins not far from Ferenczi's Miskolc.

Arnold's work has extraordinary energy and generosity which he put to use in his exploration of a humanistic psychoanalysis. In his earliest forays, he integrated Erikson's writing into the treatment of adolescents whom he recognized as needing someone to identify with in order to develop their own unique selves and, as he bumped into obstacles on his own path, he discovered and was inspired by Ferenczi in whom he found the figure whom he could take in and expand his own self.

In my collage there will photos of Arnold from the Bronx and Budapest. He will be dressed to the nines. There were times he was criticized for the boldness of his sartorial choices and, I think, not immune to being stung. But his boldness in fashion mirrored his boldness of thought and it was strength of character that allowed him to risk leaving safe, conventional paths. I treasure his inscription to me on the flyleaf of Ferenczi's book, "Keep the spirit of Ferenczi alive in your life and work."

References

Ferenczi, S. Confusion of tongues between adults and the child: The language of tenderness and passion. In M. Balint (Ed.), *Final Contributions to the Problems and Methods of Psychoanalysis*: vol. 3. New York: Brunner/Mazel, 1980, pp. 156–167, 1933.

Ferenczi, S. in John Rickman (Ed.), *First Contributions to the Theory and Technique of Psychoanalysis*: Volume 1, London: Hogarth Press, 1950.

Ferenczi, S. in John Rickman (Ed.), *Further Contributions to the Theory and Technique of Psychoanalysis*: Volume 2, London: Hogarth Press, 1952.

Ferenczi, S. in John Rickman (Ed.), *Final Contributions to the Theory and Technique of Psychoanalysis*: Volume 3, London: Hogarth Press, 1955.

Rachman, A.W. *Identity Group Psychotherapy with Adolescents*. Springfield, IL: Charles C. Thomas, 1975.

Rachman, A.W. *Sándor Ferenczi: The Psychotherapist of Tenderness and Passion*. Northvale, NJ: Jason Aronson, 1997.

Rachman, A.W. The suppression and censorship of Ferenczi's Confusion of Tongues paper. *Psychoanalytic Inquiry*, 17: 459–485, 1997b.

Rachman, A.W. Death by Silence (*Todschweigen*): The traditional method of dealing with dissidents in psychoanalysis. In R. Prince (Ed.), *The Death of Psychoanalysis: Suicide, Murder, or Rumor Greatly Exaggerated*. Northvale, NJ: Jason Aronson, pp. 154–164, 1999.

Rachman, A. W. *An "invitro" clinical study of intersubjectivity*. Presentation. *International Forum of Psychoanalysis*. Athens, Greece, October, 2010.

Rachman, A.W. Sándor Ferenczi's analysis with Elizabeth Severn: "Wild analysis" or pioneering treatment of the incest trauma. *Psychoanalytic Inquiry*, 34(2): 145–168, 2014a.

Rachman, A.W. Sándor Ferenczi as "The Bridge": My journey from phenomenology and humanistic psychotherapy to relational analysis. *Psychoanalytic Inquiry*, 34(2): 182–186, 2014b.

Rachman, A.W. Ed. *The Budapest School of Psychoanalysis: The Origin of a Two-Person Psychology and Emphatic Perspective*. London: Routledge, 2016a.

Rachman, A.W. Psychoanalysis' neglect of the incest trauma: The confusion of tongues between psychoanalysis and society. In A.W. Rachman (Ed.), *The Budapest School of Psychoanalysis: The Origin of a Two-Person Psychology and Emphatic Perspective*. London: Routledge, 2016b, pp. 164–181.

19 Arnold Wm. Rachman and the Psychoanalysis of Dissidence

Uriel García Varela

I've always considered myself a Freudian. A pluralist Freudian or – as my analyst would say – an "heterodox post-modern Freudian" (Kolteniuk, 1998) … but a Freudian, nonetheless. At sixteen, in the year 2005, I immersed myself into the world of the Unconscious through the films of David Lynch. Film led me to painting and painting led me to literature. My fascination for the oneiric through art, and through the recollection and writing of my own dreams, naturally led me to Freud's *The Interpretation of Dreams* (1900) and to psychoanalysis. From then on, I embarked on the journey of trying to understand human nature from its unconscious dimension. In addition to that, I was profoundly invested in punk rock music and the punk rock movement in the history of rock'n'roll.

This is not some random fact: little did I know that this particular element of my young spirit was something that would eventually connect me to Arnold Wm. Rachman, as a person, as an author, and as a friend. Because Rachman (2018) firmly believes that dissidence is the drive that moves a discipline forward: dissidents are the ones who question the basic foundations of science and try to reformulate them when the everchanging conditions of (inner and outer) reality confront them with their limitations. This was, of course, the case of psychoanalysis. Rachman – from his "punk rock spirit" – also explains what had happened to some analysts that became "too dissident" within the Psychoanalytic Movement: they became victims of what Rachman (2018) sharply called *Totschweigen* … they're killed by the silence of their community. That was the case of Sándor Ferenczi. But I will return to this matter later … the matter that made my quest cross with Arnold's.

When I was in college studying psychology in México, I was ambivalent. My interest in dreams aroused my interest in mental illness and mental pain, so my new goal was not only to understand the unconscious dimension of human experience, but also to help people relieve their psychic pain, starting with myself. I was convinced that the only way of healing was by understanding. Understanding being the mean to healing and healing being the final goal. This is something I still believe in seventeen years later. But, unfortunately, the University's approach was a shallow one: they were not interested in understanding or healing. Their approach to psychotherapy was to help the patient to be functional: to forget about their "irrelevant traumatic past" …

DOI: 10.4324/9781003391081-19

because it is already past, hence "it doesn't hurt anymore," and to live in the everlasting present moving towards the future. I could see the usefulness of the approach, but I couldn't accept it ... I needed something more. Psychoanalysis taught me that the traumatic past is acting permanently within us, without our knowledge; that is the nature of the Unconscious. This conviction was another point of connection with Rachman: the fundamental and constitutive importance of early trauma as etiology of psychopathology, having its consequences not only in symptomatic manifestations but in the whole psychic structure. To Rachman (2022), actual trauma does not express itself through neurotic symptoms, but through the totality of personality itself. Following Ferenczi, Rachman states:

> [In trauma] a pathological split-off nucleus (of traumatic affect, self-image, relationship interaction) develops and becomes the basis for later psychopathology by arresting and distorting moral development. This affects all subsequent development stages and tasks, including the ego function of drive regulation, reality testing, self and affect regulation, and object relations during each state.
>
> (Rachman, 2022, p. 44)

Parallel to the courses in College, I studied psychoanalysis on my own at the library: starting with classic Freud writings. Then I explored some other authors who expanded Freudian ideas in creative ways: Jacques Lacan, Heinz Hartmann, and Melanie Klein. The name of Ferenczi was only mentioned here and there. For example, in *The Ego and the Id* (1923) Freud mentions that there's a psychoanalytic hypothesis that states that human beings were forced into culture because of the catastrophes of the glacial era. In a footnote Freud writes that this hypothesis was proposed by Ferenczi in 1913 (eleven years before the publication of *"Thalassa"*). But I didn't pay much attention to these kind of details in the text. My relationship with Ferenczian thinking started a few years later.

Once I finished my major in psychology, I was eager to start formal studies in psychoanalysis. In the master's degree course in México City, we read a lot of Freud, Klein, Bion, Kernberg, and Winnicott. Ferenczi was only mentioned as a curiosity: "Freud's most brilliant disciple" but they never told us why and how. He was completely omitted from the program. Some of the teachers, when mentioning him, talked with some disdain: "He was a genius, but he became psychotic," "He was a rebel," "He did crazy experiments that Freud did not approve," "He was a dissident," and so on. As I said, by that time I hadn't read any of his papers, but those mean comments aroused my interest. I needed to know more about this "rebel analyst" ... this "punk analyst." Rachman (2018) experienced the same omission of Ferenczi when he did the psychoanalytic training in 1968. Forty years before me!

Since I couldn't find any of his books in any bookstore in México (not even online!), I had to turn my attention to the other author that was intensely in tune with my personal approach to psychoanalysis: Donald Winnicott. I became a Winnicott enthusiast and was captivated by his clinical approach, his warmness and capacity for empathy. I wrote my thesis about his clinical work with difficult patients using "therapeutic regression." The papers I focused on were "Clinical and Metapsychological Aspects of Regression in the Psycho-analytical Setting" and "Clinical Varieties of Transference," both from 1955. In dialogue with my supervisor, he told me "You should include the ideas of Michael Balint in your thesis!". Soon I bought *The Basic Fault* (1968) and read it from cover to cover in one sitting. This was, arguably, the most complete, passionate, and profound psychoanalytic writing I've ever read, from both its clinical and theoretical dimensions. Balint led me to Franz Alexander and, of course, to Ferenczi who, in fact, introduced therapeutic regression into psychoanalysis for the first time as early as 1929. I was mesmerized by his chapter about the Freud–Ferenczi misunderstanding of trauma theory. Years later I found that Rachman supports Balint's points of view but goes further: for Rachman, the Freud–Ferenczi conflict constituted a trauma for the psychoanalytic community itself. It was a Confusion of Tongues trauma from which we still have not yet recovered.

By the time I was accepted in the Institute for Psychoanalytic training, Ferenczi's books were still completely inaccessible for me. What is worse: at that time, I was in analysis with a "supposedly orthodox Freudian." He had in his library a book called "Sex and psychoanalysis" by Ferenczi, but he wouldn't let me borrow it, arguing that it would represent a "neurotic gratification" and a "violation of the setting." He told me to "associate" about my need for the book instead of borrowing it. That was torture for me. He interpreted that I wanted to strip him away from his "good objects" because I was in Oedipal rivalry with him. He said that I wanted to steal from him, to make him weak and become the king with all the treasures for myself.

The Ferenczi book incident was a minor one, a mild example of how that analyst used his overwhelming authority to exercise control over me. Other examples are more drastic: he constantly fell asleep and then denied it. When I told him about traumatic experiences in my childhood, he said that those weren't memories at all but only dreams. Perhaps the most dramatic example was when, one time, he kicked the couch and yelled that I wasn't associating properly.

To this day, I still cannot believe that someone who claimed to be an analyst made that kind of "psychoanalytic interventions" (I can only believe it because I was there, and that cruelty was aimed at me). Years later, with the help of my new warm, empathic, and awake analyst (who considers himself an "heterodox post-modern Freudian"), I could acknowledge those experiences with the previous analyst as severely traumatic.

My new analyst never doubted my experience and helped me process it. Arnold Rachman (2018) would say that I experienced Confusion of Tongues trauma with the first analyst who was keen in frustrating me and, most of all, on interpreting my feelings as "Oedipal rivalry." Rachman (2018) would also say that my new analyst used non-interpretive measures by firmly believing in my experience and by using an empathic response to my pain and frustration.

At that time, I was also fighting an ideological battle: I needed do defend psychoanalysis before my colleagues in the Psychiatric Hospital where I was working as a clinical psychologist and in the University where I was giving lectures on psychopathology. Those colleagues (Rogerian, Cognitive-behavioral, Gestalt, Systemic, etc.) claimed that psychoanalysis was not a form of psychotherapy. I even had to defend psychoanalysis as a psychotherapy before a small group of Lacanians who claimed that psychoanalysis was a method of psychic inquiry but never a means for healing. To them, in order to achieve the goal of unveiling the Unconscious, the analyst must be cold and distant, like a scientist in a laboratory.

I couldn't believe that claim. To me, *the goal of psychoanalysis is healing through the discovery of the Unconscious. And most important: that healing can only be achieved by the creation of an empathic relationship within the patient–analyst dyad.* Those Lacanians thought that my empathic approach was not a psychoanalytic one. So, for some time, I had to struggle with them, and I had to endeavor to show those colleagues that psychoanalysis is a healing and empathic form of psychotherapy. Years later, I found that Arnold Wm. Rachman (2018) proposed that there is a third rule in psychoanalysis. The first rule, established by Freud (1900), is free association; the second one, established by Ferenczi (1928), is the analysis of the analyst; and the third one, proposed also by Ferenczi (1928), but recovered and stressed by Rachman (2018), is the rule of empathy. Rachman even exposes how authors like Heinz Kohut were part of the *Totschweigen* campaign against Ferenczi by not acknowledging him as the one who introduced empathy to *psychoanalysis*.

One day I had a lucky strike. I was browsing in a bookstore called *El Sótano* (The Basement), and I found a treasure. The title read: *Sin simpatía no hay curación: El diario clínico de 1932* by Sándor Ferenczi. I could not believe my eyes. I must clarify that in Latin America our title for the *Clinical Diary* is the same as the German edition from 1988: *Ohne Sympathie keine Heilung: Das klinische tagebuch von 1932.* The title itself condensed my personal approach to psychoanalysis and consolidated my drive to know more about this enigmatic author. I must confess that, when I brought the book home and started reading it, I hardly understood a word. In part because the translation had some kind of Lacanian bias and in part because the text itself, being a personal journal, was sort of disjointed, which amplifies the mysterious nature of the text. What drew my attention right away was the constant use of the word "Mutuality." I understood, from the very beginning of my reading, that Ferenczi's model of the mind was that of a co-construction.

In the *Clinical Diary* I found what I considered the four core concepts of Ferenczian metapsychology: (1) Human beings mostly communicate from our primitive unconscious dimension (what Ferenczi called "Dialogue of Unconsciouses" (p. 84). (2) Unconscious communication between the baby and the mother builds the psychic apparatus (creates that of the baby and transforms that of the mother ... they influence each other). (3) When the adult doesn't handle their own mental life, they place their unbearable psychic contents into the child's mind by intropression and "alien transplants" (p. 81); this constitutes trauma. And (4) The healing process can only be achieved through regression and rebuilding of the psyche by the analytic pair, that is analogue to the baby–mother relationship. The severely damaged patient needs a maternal object, and the analyst must let himself be the mother. Since trauma is an interpsychic process (not intrapsychic), psychoanalysis and healing must also be interpsychic in nature.

The part of the *Diary* that moved me the most was, of course, the case of R.N. Not because of the therapeutic experiment of mutual analysis but because of the Ferenczian notion of mutuality (in psychic development, in psychoanalytic treatment, and in all human interaction). I found the most dramatic example of this phenomenon in the entry of February 20:

> Continuing discontent [by R.N.], dissatisfaction with the results of the preoccupation with traumatic events, even though most intensively pursued, over many hours ....
>
> Acting on a sudden impulse ..., I warn the patient that I must tell her something that one does not usually tell patients – is she strong enough to listen to me? In fact, she must be, otherwise she would not have asked me for mutual openness. – With great resolve, the patient demands absolute frankness, whereupon I tell her that in fact I deliberately exaggerated when I continually spoke of the success expected from her analysis. In reality I am often afraid that the whole treatment will go wrong and that she will end up insane or commit suicide ... The result was, quite unexpectedly, complete appeasement: "If at the time I had been able to bring my father such a confession of the truth and to realize the dangerousness of the situation, I could have saved my sanity."
>
> (Ferenczi, 1932, pp. 37–38)

To me, this wasn't a confession of countertransference for the sake of it: it was, as Rachman would say, a therapeutic self-disclosure (2018). With his non-interpretive intervention, Ferenczi acted differently from the father of R.N.'s childhood, breaking the denial and the disavowal, and giving her the sense of reality needed to cope with trauma.

As I kept on reading the *Diary*, I understood that R.N. and Ferenczi were working as a truly analytic pair, communicating from -what I later called- the *Mutuality Principle* of the psychic apparatus (García Varela, 2023). I needed to know more about this brilliant, fascinating, and wounded woman whose real name was Elizabeth Severn.

A few years later, a dear patient of mine, who knew I was interested in Ferenczi – and for whom I feel infinite gratitude – gave me the most amazing Christmas present: an original 1955 Hogarth Press copy of *Final Contributions to the Problems and Methods of Psycho-Analysis*. I read it in its entirety on a ten-hour flight and my passion for Ferenczi grew even more. In that compilation (edited by non-other than Michel Balint) Ferenczi names Severn twice. First, in "The Principle of Relaxation and Neocatharsis" (1929), he says:

> For this notion [psychotic splitting off] I am partly indebted to discoveries made by our colleague, Elizabeth Severn, which she personally communicated to me.
>
> (p. 122)

So, Severn was not only a patient, but a colleague who collaborated directly with Ferenczi. Then, in "Child-Analysis in the Analysis of Adults" (1931) he stated:

> Our colleague, Elizabeth Severn, who is doing a training-analysis with me, once pointed out to me … that I sometimes disturbed the spontaneity of the fantasy-production with my questions and answers. … [My interventions] should compel the patient to continue the work by his own extensions.
>
> (p. 133)

I found that Severn was, in fact, training with Ferenczi to become an analyst herself. Ferenczi acknowledges her contributions and shows huge respect for her in his own writings. My final stage to becoming a full Ferenczi enthusiast came with two events: my long-awaited acquisition of the *Complete Works of Sándor Ferenczi* (the ones compiled into four volumes by Judith Dupont in the 1960s. Of course, I've got the Spanish edition that was translated from French), which I bought from an underground old-book dealer in a very dangerous neighborhood in México City. And finally, my reading of Arnold Wm. Rachman's *Elizabeth Severn: The Evil Genius of Psychoanalysis* (2018). His influence was so powerful that I can even feel it (as you can see) in my writing style. With every chapter you can see the passion of a man who bears his soul in his unwavering quest to give voice to those who were silenced. His endeavor is to bring back Ferenczi and Severn from *Totschweigen*. On one occasion – as he tells in his book – he "ma[d]e a silent pledge to [him]self: Arnold, *never again remain* silent when someone privately or publicly attacks Ferenczi" (Rachman, 2018, p. 64). He is, as I stated in the title, the psychoanalyst of dissidents.

In Arnold's book I found that, before her analysis with Ferenczi, Severn (whose birth name was Leota Loretta Brown) was an experienced psychotherapist, author of three books about her field, a pioneer of active therapy (even before Ferenczi), a scholar of Freud, Putnam, Langue, and Williams James, and a committed explorer of the Unconscious with her own psychoanalytic perspective. I also found that at the beginning of her treatment with Ferenczi, she went to visit Freud, just to discover that he wasn't keen on the healing part of psychoanalysis. That's why she chose Ferenczi over Freud. Arnold's book consolidated my will to write my PhD thesis on "The Implicit Theory of

Mutuality in Sándor Ferenczi's Work," which can only be explored through the dyad Ferenczi–Severn.

Thanks to my friends Luis Martín Cabré, Carlos Castillo, and the Spanish group I had the opportunity to be involved directly in the International Ferenczi Community. In June 2023 I presented a paper in the Conference of Budapest. There I met Arnold for the first time. I was so excited to finally meet him in person. During the Q&A part of his lecture I asked if he thought that psychoanalytic empathy (*Einfühlung* in German) has to do with a sort of temporary symbiotic fusion between patient and analyst. He told me: "Not a fusion, but an attunement." A few hours later I went to him to present myself. He was kind and warm from the very beginning. The first thing he said to me was "Of course I remember you, you're the *Einfühlung* young man." We talked daily throughout the days of the Conference, and we exchanged email addresses. He told me that we should keep our dialogue and work together.

Once I was back in México, I thought that perhaps he was only being polite, and he wasn't serious about us collaborating. After a week I sent him an email, to which he responded immediately:

Dear Uriel: I'm so happy that you wrote to me. I tried so many times to write to you, but the emails kept on returning! Now I see I misspelled your email address! Looking forward for our collaborating together. Warmly. A.

Since then, we've been meeting once every two weeks via Zoom; exchanging ideas, dialoguing, and preparing the Sándor Ferenczi Mexican Study Group and other projects.

Arnold encourages my creativity and my curiosity. At the beginning of this paper, I stated that he has a "punk rock" approach to psychoanalysis. That is, amongst other things, because he is passionately reaching for the truth. When listening to him or reading one of his writings I remember Joe Strummer from The Clash saying, "We're sick of the bullshit. Give us some truth. That's the energy of punk rock. But don't get me wrong, it's a hard way to live" (Hayden, 2000). This was also stated by John Lennon: "All I want is the truth … just gimme some truth." He, like Arnold, was a champion of giving voice to the dissidents (and he also lived in New York). I must add that Arnold is also a collage artist, the punk rock art by excellence, inherited by dadaism. We just need to compare Arnold's art to the 1970s' flyers to announce the punk rock shows at the CBGB in New York.

Thanks to Arnold my passion for Ferenczi and psychoanalysis is fully consolidated. I don't know … maybe it is time to consider myself a Ferenczian.

References

Balint, M. *The Basic Fault*. Evanston, IL: Northwestern University Press, 1968.

Ferenczi, S. The elasticity of psycho-analytic technique. In *Final Contributions to the Problems and Methods of Psychoanalysis*. London: Hogarth Press, 1928.

Ferenczi, S. The principle of relaxation and neocatharsis. In *Final Contributions to the Problems and Methods of Psychoanalysis*. London: Hogarth Press, 1929.

Ferenczi, S. Child-analysis in the analysis of adults. In *Final Contributions to the Problems and Methods of Psychoanalysis*. London: Hogarth Press, 1931.

Ferenczi, S. *The Clinical Diary of Sándor Ferenczi*. EE.UU. Cambridge, MA: Harvard University Press, 1932/1988.

Ferenczi, S. *Sin simpatía no hay curación. El diario clínico de 1932*. Buenos Aires: Amorrortu, 1932[1997].

Ferenczi, S. *Final Contributions to the Problems and Methods of Psychoanalysis*. London: Hogarth Press, 1955.

Ferenczi, S. *Ohne Sympathies keine Heilung. Das klinische Tagebuch von 1932*. Frankfurt: Fischer Taschenbuch Verlag, 1988.

Freud, S. *La interpretación de los sueños* en *Obras completas* IV. Buenos Aires: Amorrortu, 1900.

Freud, S. *El yo y el ello* en *Obras completas* XIX. Buenos Aires: Amorrortu, 1923.

García Varela, U. *The notion of Mutuality throughout the works of Sándor Ferenczi*. Presented at the *13th International Sándor Ferenczi Conference, Budapest*, June 9–11, 2023. [Manuscript submitted for publication], 2023.

Hayden, C. Legacy: Joe Strummer. In *Penthouse*, June 2000.

Kolteniuk, M. Las relaciones de objeto a la luz del freudiano perdido. In *Cuadernos de Psicoanálisis*, XXXI: 1–2, January–June 1998. Asociación Psicoanalítica Mexicana, 1998.

Lennon, J. *Gimme some Truth*. On *Imagine* [LP]. Capitol Records, 1971.

Rachman, A.W. *Elizabeth Severn: The "Evil Genius" of Psychoanalysis*. New York: Routledge, 2018.

Rachman, A.W. *Psychoanalysis and Society's Neglect of the Sexual Abuse of Children, Youth and Adults. Re-addressing Freud's Original Theory of Sexual Abuse and Trauma*. New York: Routledge, 2022.

Winnicott, D.W. Clinical varieties of transference. In *Through Paediatrics to Psychoanalysis*. Brunner Routledge, 1955.

Winnicott, D.W. Metapsychological and clinical aspects of regression within the psycho-analytical set-up. In *Through Paediatrics to Psychoanalysis*. London: Routledge, 1955.

20 Awards, Honors, Publications, and Courses

Arnold Wm. Rachman PhD

Awards and Honors

- Dean's list. Senior Semester University of Buffalo, Buffalo, New York, 1960.
- United States Public Health Fellowship in Research Methods. Graduate School University of Chicago, 1962–1964.
- National Institute in Mental Health Postdoctoral Fellowship. Postgraduate Center in Mental Health, New York City, 1964–1966.
- Postgraduate Center For Mental Health Institute Award for the Outstanding Original Paper on the Psychoanalysis of a Child or Adolescent, 1970.
- Postgraduate Center For Mental Health Institute Award for the Outstanding Paper on Individual Psychoanalysis, 1975.
- Postgraduate Center For Mental Health Institute Award for the Outstanding Original Paper on Analysis in Groups, 1985. (Arnold Wm. Rachman was one of only two members of the Postgraduate Center For Mental Health Institute to win all three awards sponsored by the Postgraduate Center (the other award recipient was Henry Kellerman, PhD)).
- CCOMMI Mental Health Exchange Worships, Tel Aviv, Israel, 1976. Award In Appreciation of Participation in the Israel/United States Workshops.
- Award to Arnold Wm. Rachman, PhD with Appreciation and Gratitude, the Postgraduate Psychoanalytic Society, September 23, 2011.
- Sándor Ferenczi Award, best published work in the realm of psychoanalysis related to trauma and dissociation in the past 24 months. International Society for the Study of Trauma and Dissociation, 2023.

Sándor Ferenczi Bibliography

A complete list of conference presentations, articles and courses taught about Sándor Ferenczi, Elizabeth Severn, and The Budapest School of Psychoanalysis, starting with Arnold Rachman's first article about Sándor Ferenczi published in 1977 until 2024, a total of 47 years.

DOI: 10.4324/9781003391081-20

Presentations, Papers, and Courses

Rachman, A.W. (1965). The Affect Cognition Scale in measuring the outcome of psychotherapy. Doctoral Dissertation. The Counseling and Psychotherapy Research Center. University of Chicago.

Rachman, A.W. (1977a). Interviews with Dr. Sándor Lorand about Dr. Sándor Ferenczi. October 4, 1977, and December 27, 1977.

Rachman, A.W. (1977b). Sándor Ferenczi: the father of active and humanistic psychoanalysis. Invited Lecture. Fellowship training Program. Postgraduate Center For Mental Health. New York City, March.

Rachman, A.W. (1978). The first encounter session: Ferenczi's case of the female Croatian Musician. Presentation. American Psychotherapy Association Convention, New Orleans, LA, February.

Rachman, A.W. (1980). The role of activity in psychodynamic psychotherapy. Invited Lecture Series. Pine Rest Christian Hospital. Grand Rapids, Michigan. April.

Rachman, A.W. (1981). Humanistic analysis in groups. *Psychotherapy: Theory, Research and Practice*, 18(4): 457–477.

Rachman, A.W. (1984a). Freud and Ferenczi: the twenty-five year relationship that changed the course of psychoanalysis. Postgraduate Center Psychoanalytic Society. New York City, February.

Rachman, A.W. (1984b). An outline of a Ferenczian psychoanalysis. Presentation. Postgraduate Center Psychoanalytic Society. New York City, March.

Rachman, A.W. (1986). The rule of empathy. Sándor Ferenczi's pioneering contributions to the empathic method is psychoanalysis. Presentation. American Academy of Psychoanalysis. New York City, December.

Rachman, A.W. (1987a). Confusion of tongues: the Ferenczian metaphor for childhood seduction and emotional trauma. Presentation. American Academy of Psychoanalysis. Chicago, Ill. May 8.

Rachman, A.W. (1987b). The concept of evil in psychoanalysis. Discussant Robert Lifton's paper "The evil of the Nazi doctors." Postgraduate Center For Mental Health. November.

Rachman, A.W. (1988a). The rule of empathy. Sándor Ferenczi's pioneering contribution to the empathic method in psychoanalysis. *Journal of the American Academy of Psychoanalysis*, 16(1):1–27. January.

Rachman, A.W. (1988b). Liberating the creative self through active combined psychotherapy. In N. Slavinska-Holy (Ed.), *Borderline and Narcissistic Patients in Therapy*. New York: New York. International Universities Press.

Rachman, A.W. (1988c). Sándor Ferenczi's influence in modern psychoanalysis. Presentation. History of Psychoanalysis Course. Institute For Modern Psychoanalysis. New York City, February.

Rachman, A.W. (1988d). Sándor Ferenczi's contributions to modern psychoanalysis. Presentation. Institute for Modern Psychoanalysis. New York City. March.

Rachman, A.W. (1989a). Confusion of tongues: the Ferenczian metaphor for childhood seduction and emotional trauma. *Journal of the American Academy of Psychoanalysis*, 17(2): 182–205.

Rachman, A.W. (1989b). Ferenczi and contemporary psychoanalysis. Course. Psychoanalytic Institute. Postgraduate Center for Mental Health. New York City, Fall Semester.

Rachman, A.W. (1989c). Sándor Ferenczi and Contemporary Psychoanalysis. Course. Psychoanalytic Institute. Postgraduate Center for Mental Health. Fall Semester, NYC.

Rachman, A.W. (1989d). Ferenczi's contribution to the evolution of a Self-Psychology framework in psychoanalysis. In Detrich and Detrich, S.P. (Eds.), *Self Psychology: Comparison and Contrast*, pp. 81–100. Hillsdale, NY: Analytic Press.

Rachman, A.W. (1989e). Sándor Ferenczi: Psychoanalysis's fallen angel (unpublished).

Rachman, A.W. (1990a). Countertransference issues in the treatment of sexual trauma by group analysis. Paper presented. Postgraduate Center For Mental Health, New York City, March.

Rachman, A.W. (1990b). Ferenczi's clinical contributions. Seminar. Private practice. New York City, January–May.

Rachman, A.W. (1990c). Ferenczi and Jung: kindred spirits. Presentation. C.G. Jung Foundation of New York City. January 27.

Rachman, A.W. and Fenster, A. and Wiedemann, C.F. (1990). The investigation of a psychoanalyst pioneer: empirical data on the clinical work of Sándor Ferenczi. *Psychotherapy*, 27(4): 547–552.

Rachman, A.W. and Fenster, A. and Wiedemann, C.F. (1992). The relationship between experience as a therapist, age, and beliefs about psychotherapeutic functioning. *Psychoanalysis and Psychotherapy*, 11(2): 115–126.

Rachman, A.W. (1991a). An oedipally conflicted patient. In A. Wolf and L. Kutash (Eds.), *Psychotherapy of the Submerged Personality*, pp. 215–238. Northvale, NJ: Jason Aronson.

Rachman, A.W. (1991b). Ferenczi's early treatment of a female homosexual transvestite: the case of Rosa K.: (1902) (unpublished). July.

Rachman, A.W. (1991c). An analysand's "Aura of Ferenczi". Psychoanalytic session. November 15 (unpublished).

Rachman, A.W. (1991d). Psychoanalysis, sexual seduction and the contemporary analysis of Incest. Presentation. American Academy of Psychoanalysis. New York City, December 19.

Rachman, A.W. (1992a). Ferenczi's discovery of confusion of tongues theory. Presentation. American Psychological Association. Philadelphia, PA. April.

Rachman, A.W. (1992b). Ferenczi's clinical diary. Presentation. American Academy of Psychoanalysis. Washington, D.C. May.

Rachman, A.W. (1992c). The confusion of tongues between Hedda Nussbaum and Joel Steinberg: dynamics of an abusive relationship. Presentation. International Conference of the Psycho-Historical Society. John Jay College. New York City. June.

Rachman, A.W. (1993a). Ferenczi and sexuality. In L. Aron and A. Harris (Eds.), *The Theoretical and Clinical Contributions of Sándor Ferenczi*, pp. 81–100. Hillsdale, NJ: Analytic Press.

Rachman, A.W. (1993b). Sándor Ferenczi's contributions to psychoanalysis. Seminar. National Institute for the Psychotherapies. New York City, January 9.

Rachman, A.W. (1993c). Ferenczi's confusion of tongues theory. Presentation. Modern Psychoanalytic Institute. January 19.

Rachman, A.W. (1993d). The evil of childhood seduction. Presentation. American Academy of Psychoanalysis. December, New York City.

Rachman, A.W. (1993e). The validation of the incest trauma. Presentation. Group Analysis. Eastern Group Psychotherapy Association. November 14, NYC.

Rachman, A.W. (1994a). The confusion of tongues theory: Ferenczi's legacy to psychoanalysis. In A. Haynal and E. Falzeder (Eds.), *100 Years of Psychoanalysis*, pp. 235–255. London: Karnac.

Rachman, A.W. (1994b). *Non-interpretive Behavior by the Psychoanalyst in the Psychoanalytic Situation*. Ferenczi Symposium. IX Forum of International Federation of Psychoanalytic Societies. Florence, Italy, May 14.

Rachman, A.W. (1994c). Sándor Ferenczi and Michael Balint. Course. Object Relations Institute. Spring. New York City.

Rachman, A.W. (1994d). Ferenczi's relaxation-principle (*Nachgiebigkeit*): the origins or non-interpretive behavior in IX Psychoanalysis Forum. International Forum of Psychoanalysis. Florence, Italy. May 14.

Rachman, A.W. (1994e). Ferenczi's humanistic psychoanalysis: the challenge for analytic treatment in the 21st century. Presentation. Encontro Internacional Perspectivas
Psicanaliticas. São Paulo, Brazil. August 16.

Rachman, A.W. (1994f). Oedipus From Brooklyn: a Ferenczian analysis. Presentation.
Circulo Brasiliano de Psicanálise. Belo Horozonte, Brazil. August 18.

Rachman, A.W. and Mattick (1994). The confusion of tongues between Freud and
Dora: The need for tenderness not sexuality (unpublished).

Rachman, A.W. (1995a). Theoretical issues in the treatment of childhood sexual
trauma in SCI patients: the Confusion of Tongues theory of childhood seduction. *SCI
Psychological Process*, 8(1): 20–25. February.

Rachman, A.W. (1995b). The confusion of tongues between adolescents and adults:
communication and interaction in adolescent group psychotherapy. Presentation.
Fourth Annual Conference Missouri Group Psychotherapy Society. St. Louis, MO.
Friday, April 7.

Rachman, A.W. (1995c). Ferenczi's reformulation of the seduction theory. Presentation.
Psychoanalytic Society of Campinas. Campinas, Brazil. August 19.

Rachman, A.W. (1995d). Sándor Ferenczi's pioneering contributions to the analysis of
the incest trauma. Plenary Presentation. First Ferenczi Congress of Latin America.
São Paulo, Brazil. Sunday, August 28.

Rachman, A.W. (1995e). Ferenczi's Relaxation Principle (*Nachgiebigkeit*) as an ante-
cedent to the concept of optimal responsiveness (unpublished).

Rachman, A.W. and Menaker, E. (1995). Ferenczi and Rank. Course. Training and
Research Institute For Self-Psychology. Spring Semester.

Rachman, A.W. (1996a). The confusion of tongues between Sigmund Freud and Anna
Freud: issues of seduction. Eighth Biennial Conference, Psychoanalytic Society,
NYU Postdoctoral Program. New York City. February 3.

Rachman, A.W. (1996b). The Ferenczi Renaissance. Discussion of G. Galdi's paper:
The terrorism of suffering: the Clinical Diary of Sándor Ferenczi revisited. Karen
Horney Psycho-analytic Institute and Center. Thursday. April 11.

Rachman, A.W. (1996c). The evolution of the concept of clinical empathy: from
Ferenczi to Kohut. Presentation. 19th Annual Conference Association of Analytic
Self Psychology. Washington, D.C. October 20.

Rachman, A.W. (1996d). A contemporary model for the Budapest School of
Psychoanalysis and Psychotherapy. Grand Rapids Seminars. Grand Rapids, MI.
November.

Rachman, A.W. (1996e). Countertransference analysis and the subjective experience
of the analyst (unpublished).

Rachman, A.W. (1996f). Ferenczi and Rank. Course. Training and Research Center for
Self-Psychology. February 9–May 31.

Rachman, A.W. (1997a). The suppression and censorship of Ferenczi's Confusion of
Tongues paper. *Psychoanalytic Inquiry*, 17(4), December.

Rachman, A.W. (1997b). Sándor Ferenczi's contributions to the evolution of a self-psychology framework in psychoanalysis. *Progress in Self Psychology*, 14. New York:
Analytic Press.

Rachman, A.W. (1997c). Analyst's self-disclosure: the search for authenticity in the
psychoanalytic situation. Presentation. 20th Annual International Conference on
the Psychology of the Self. Chicago, Ill. November 16.

Rachman, A.W. (1997d). Discussant. Giselle Galdi's "The terrorism of suffering": The
Clinical Diary of Sándor Ferenczi revisited. *American Journal of Psychoanalysis*,
57(1): 80–85.

Rachman, A.W. (1998a). Ferenczi's "Relaxation-Principle" and the contemporary clinical practice of psychoanalysis. G. Galdi (Ed.) Ferenczi Number. *American Journal
of Psychoanalysis*, 68(1): 63–81.

Rachman, A.W. (1998b). "Self-Psychology developed in the spirit of Sándor Ferenczi" (Ernest Wolf): the relationship between The Budapest School and the Psychology of the Self Orientation. Presentation. Sándor Ferenczi International Conference – "Ferenczi and Contemporary Psychoanalysis". Madrid, Spain. Friday, March 6.

Rachman, A.W. (1998c). Judicious self-disclosure by the psychoanalyst. International Forum of *Psychoanalysis*, 7(4): 263–269, December.

Rachman, A.W. (1998d). Ferenczi and Rank. Course. Training and Research Center for Self-Psychology. Spring Semester.

Rachman, A.W. (1999a). Death by Silence (*Totschweigen*): The traditional method of silencing the dissidents of psychoanalysis. In R.M. Prince (Ed.), *The Death of Psychoanalysis: Murder, Suicide, or Rumor Greatly Exaggerated?* pp. 153–163. Northvale, NJ: Jason Aronson.

Rachman, A.W. (1999b). Ferenczi's rise and fall from analytic grace: The Ferenczi Renaissance revisited. *Group*, 23(4): 103–119.

Rachman, A.W. (1999c). Sándor Ferenczi's ideas and methods and their relevance to group psychotherapy. *Group*, 23(3–4H): 121–144.

Rachman, A.W. (1999d). Ferenczi's rise and fall from "analytic grace": The Ferenczi Renaissance revisited. *Group*, 23(3–4): 103–119.

Rachman, A.W. (2000a). The search for authenticity in the psychoanalytic situation. Presentation. XI Forum, International Federation of Psychoanalytic Societies, May, New York City.

Rachman, A.W. (2000b). Ferenczi's Confusion of Tongues theory and the analysis of the incest trauma. *Psychoanalytic Social Work*, 7(1): 27–53.

Rachman, A.W. (2000c). Issues of power, control and status. From Ferenczi to Foucault. *Group: Journal of Eastern Group Psychotherapy*, 7(1): 121–144.

Rachman, A.W. (2001). Sándor Ferenczi as a role model for contemporary psychoanalysts. Arizona Group Psychotherapy Society Newsletter. May/June.

Rachman, A.W. (2002a). Beyond neutrality: The curative function of analyst self-disclosure in the psychoanalytic situation. In J. Reppen, M.A. Schulman, and J. Tucker (Eds.), *Way beyond Freud: Postmodern Psychoanalysis Evaluated*. London: Open Gate.

Rachman, A.W. (2002b). The resolution of an erotic transference in group psychotherapy. Presentation. American Group Psychotherapy Association Conference. February, New Orleans, LA.

Rachman, A.W. and Mattick, P. (2002). Freud's "confusion of tongues": issues of power, control and status in the analysis of Dora (unpublished).

Rachman, A.W. (2003b). Freud's analysis of his daughter Anna: A Confusion of Tongues. In A. Roland, B. Ulanov, and C. Babre (Eds.), *Creative Dissent: Psychoanalysis in Evolution*, pp. 59–71. Westport, CT: Preager.

Rachman, A.W. (2003c). Issues of power, control, and status in group interaction: from Ferenczi to Foucault. *Group*, 27(2–3): 89–105. September.

Rachman, A.W. (2003d). *Psychotherapy of Difficult Cases: Flexibility and Responsiveness in Contemporary Clinical Practice*. Madison, CT: Psychosocial Press.

Rachman, A.W. (2004). The role of childhood sexual seduction in the development of an erotic transference: perversion in the psychoanalytic situation. Presentation. XIII International Forum of Psychoanalysis. Belo Horizonte, Brazil, August 24–28.

Rachman, A.W. (2004a). Beyond neutrality: the creative function of analyst self-disclosure in the psychoanalytic situation. In J. Reppen, M.A. Schulman, and J. Tucker (Eds.), *Way Beyond Freud: Postmodern Psychoanalysis Evaluated*. London: The Open Gate Press.

Rachman, A.W. (2004b). A Confusion of Tongues in supervision (unpublished).

Rachman, A.W. and Kennedy, R. and Yard, M. (2005). Erotic transference and the relationship to childhood sexual seduction: perversion in the psychoanalytic situation. *International Forum of Psychoanalysis*, 14(3–4): 183–187.

Rachman, A.W. and Hutton, L. (2006). Clinical flexibility in the psychoanalytic situation: "The elasticity principle". *Psychoanalytic Social Work*, 13(1): 21–42.
Rachman, A.W. (2006). From phenomenology and humanistic psychotherapy to the Budapest School of Psychoanalysis to Relational Psychoanalysis. Invited Address. Postgraduate Psychoanalytic Society. New York City, December.
Rachman, A.W. (2007a). Sándor Ferenczi's contributions to the evolution of psychoanalysis. *Psychoanalytic Psychology*, 24(1): 74–96.
Rachman, A.W. (2007b). The road to creative dissidents. Sándor Ferenczi's clinical journey and the evolution of psychoanalysis. Invited Address. Postgraduate Psychoanalytic Society – Friday Evening Series "Learning From Our Past", New York City.
Rachman, A.W. and Kennedy, R.E. and Yard, M.A. (2009). Erotic transference and its relationship to childhood seduction. *Psychoanalytic Social Work*, 16: 12–30.
Rachman, A.W. and Yard, M.A., and Kennedy, R.E. (2009b). Non-interpretive measures in the analysis of trauma. *Psychoanalytic Psychology*, 26(3): 259–273.
Rachman, A.W. (2010a). An "invitro" study of intersubjectivity: The analysis of Mrs. Elizabeth Severn with Dr. Sándor Ferenczi. Presentation: International Forum of Psychoanalysis. Athens, Greece.
Rachman, A.W. (2010b). The origins of a relational perspective in the ideas of Sándor Ferenczi and the Budapest School of Psychoanalysis. *Psychoanalytic Perspectives*, 7(1): 43–60.
Rachman, A.W. (2010c). Sándor Ferenczi's analysis of Elizabeth Severn; "Wild Analysis" or pioneering attempt to analyze the incest trauma.
Rachman, A.W. (2011). The discovery of Mrs. Elizabeth Severn's Paper. Invited Presentation. Postgraduate Psychoanalytic Society. New York City, September 23.
Rachman, A.W. (2012a). Psychodynamics of abduction: The Confusion of Tongues Trauma. Presentation. The International Forum for Psychoanalysis, Mexico City, Mexico. October.
Rachman, A.W. (2012b). The analysis of the incest trauma: from the Seduction Hypothesis to the Confusion of Tongues Trauma. Presentation. The First Annual Sándor Ferenczi Seminars. The Hungarian House. New York City. Saturday, November 17.
Rachman, A.W. (2012c). The Confusion of Tongues between Sándor Ferenczi and Elizabeth Severn. Plenary Presentation. The International Sándor Ferenczi Conference, "Faces of Trauma". Budapest, Hungary, Saturday, June 3.
Rachman, A.W. (2012d). The relational dimension in psychoanalysis: From Ferenczi to Mitchell. Presentation. The Czech Psychoanalytic Society. Prague, The Czech Republic, Saturday, May 26.
Rachman, A.W. and Mattick, P. (2012). The Confusion of Tongues in the psychoanalytic relationship. *Psychoanalytic Social Work*, 19(1–2): 167–190.
Rachman, A.W. (2013). Arnold Wm. Rachman's discussion with Professor Martin Bergmann. Freud/Ferenczi Narrative. Presentation. New York City. November 13.
Rachman, A.W. (2014a). The "evil genius" of psychoanalysis: Elizabeth Severn, Dr. Sándor Ferenczi's partner in the pioneering study of trauma, The Library of Congress, Washington, D.C., June 2. Webcast-www.loc.gov.
Rachman, A.W. (2014b). Sándor Ferenczi's analysis with Elizabeth Severn: "Wild analysis" or pioneering treatment of the incest trauma. In A.W. Rachman (Ed.), *Sándor Ferenczi's Contributions to the Evolution of the Theory and Technique in Psychoanalysis*. *Psychoanalytic Inquiry*, 34(2): 145–168.
Rachman, A.W. (2014c). Elizabeth Severn: Sándor Ferenczi's analysand, colleague and collaborator in the study of trauma. In A. Harris and S. Kuchuck (Eds.), *The Legacy of Sándor Ferenczi*, Vol. II: From Ghost to Ancestor. London: Routledge.

Rachman, A.W. (2014d). Sándor Ferenczi as the bridge: My journey from phenomenology and humanistic psychotherapy to relational analysis. In A.W. Rachman (Ed.) Sándor Ferenczi's contributions to the evolution of the theory and technique in psychoanalysis. *Psychoanalytic Inquiry*, 34(2).

Rachman, A.W. (2015). Elizabeth Severn: From initiative, self-taught therapist, to psychoanalyst and Sándor Ferenczi's mutual analytic partner. Presentation. The Sándor Ferenczi Center at The New School of Social Research, NYC, September 19, 2015.

Rachman, A.W. (2016a). Psychoanalysis's neglect of the incest trauma: The Confusion of Tongues between psychoanalysis and society. In. Rachman, A.W. (Ed.). The Budapest School of Psychoanalysis. London: Routledge, pp. 164–181.

Rachman, A.W. (2016b). Confusion of tongues trauma in child abduction: Revising the Stockholm Syndrome. In A.W. Rachman (Ed.), *The Budapest School of Psychoanalysis*, pp. 182–208. London: Routledge.

Rachman, A.W. (2017a). The donation of the Elizabeth Severn Papers to the Ferenczi House, Budapest, Hungary. March 1.

Rachman, A.W. (2017b). Elizabeth Severn, the "evil genius" of psychoanalysis. Sándor Ferenczi Seminars. Florence Italy. July.

Rachman, A.W. (2018a). *Totschweigen* (Death by Silence): Removal of Elizabeth Severn's ideas and work from mainstream psychoanalysis. In A.W. Rachman, *Elizabeth Severn: The "Evil Genius" of Psychoanalysis*, pp. 57–70. London: Routledge.

Rachman, A.W. (2018b). The Uncovering of a Lost Psychoanalytic Legacy: The Papers of Elizabeth Severn. Presentation. The International Sándor Ferenczi Conference. Florence, Italy. May.

Rachman, A.W. (2019a). Elizabeth Severn as a person, clinician and collaborator of Sándor Ferenczi. Presentation. The Irish Psychoanalytic Society. Dún Laoghaire, Ireland. May 11.

Rachman, A.W. (2019b). The Confusion of Tongues: Sándor Ferenczi and the Budapest School of Psychoanalysis: Revolutionary Paradigm Shift for Psychoanalysis. Presentation. Irish Psychoanalytic Society. Dún Laoghaire, Ireland. May 10.

Rachman, A.W. (2019c). A contemporary view of Freud's Case of the Wolf Man/Sergei Pankejeff: New evidence of sexual abuse. International Psychoanalytic Association (unpublished).

Rachman, A.W. (2019d). Sándor Ferenczi's contributions to psychoanalysis. Course. Postgraduate Psychoanalytic Institute. New York City. Winter Semester.

Rachman, A.W. (2020). The contributions of Sándor Ferenczi to the origins of Relational Psychoanalysis. Course. Postgraduate Psychoanalytic Institute. New York City. Spring Semester.

Rachman, A.W. (2021). My traumatic journey toward becoming a psychoanalyst: From phenomenology and Person-Centered Psychotherapy to Sándor Ferenczi and the Budapest School of Psychoanalysis to Relational Psychoanalysis. In A.W. Rachman and H. Kooden (Eds.), *Different Paths Towards Becoming a Psychoanalyst and Psychotherapist: Personal Passions, Subjective Experiences and Unusual Journeys*. London: Routledge.

Rachman, A.W. (2023a). Elizabeth Severn: Sándor Ferenczi's "Mutual Analytic Partner". Presentation. 150th Anniversary Sándor Ferenczi Conference. Budapest, Hungary.

Rachman, A.W. (2023b). The establishment of the Elizabeth Severn Section of the Sándor Ferenczi Archives, The Sándor Ferenczi House, Budapest, Hungary. Presentation. The Opening of The Elizabeth Severn Archives, Sándor Ferenczi's Villa, Budapest, Hungary.

Rachman, A.W. and Mucci, C. (2023). *Ferenczi's Confusion of Tongues Theory of Trauma: A Neurobiological Perspective*. London: Routledge.

Rachman, A.W. and García Verila, U. (2023–2024). Mexican Psychoanalytic Sándor Ferenczi Study Group (Via Zoom). October, 2023–July, 2024.

Rachman, A.W. (2024). Child sexual abuse and psychoanalytic theory: Sigmund Freud and Sándor Ferenczi's childhood seduction. In W. Middleton and M.J. Dorahy (Eds.), *Contemporary Perspectives on Freud's Seduction Theory and Psychoanalysis: Revisiting Masson's "The Assault on Truth"*. London: Routledge.

Books

Rachman, A.W. (1997). *Sándor Ferenczi: The Psychotherapist of Tenderness and Passion*. Northvale, NJ: Jason Aronson.

Rachman, A.W. (2003). *Psychotherapy of Difficult Cases: Flexibility and Responsiveness in Clinical Practice*. Madison, CT. Psychosocial Press.

Rachman, A.W. and Klett, S. (2015). *Analysis of the Incest Trauma: Retrieval, Recovery, Renewal*. London: Karnac.

Rachman, A.W. (Ed.) (2016a). *The Budapest School of Psychoanalysis: The Origin of a Two-Person Psychology And Empathic Perspective*. London: Routledge.

Rachman, A.W. (2016b). The Acquisition, Restoration and Donation of the Elizabeth Severn Papers: A lot legacy of psychoanalysis (unpublished).

Rachman, A.W. (2018). *Elizabeth Severn: The "Evil Genius" of Psychoanalysis*. London: Routledge.

Rachman, A.W. and Kooden, H. (Eds.). (2021). *Different Paths towards Becoming a Psychoanalyst and Psychotherapist: Personal Passions, Subjective Experiences and Unusual Journey*. London: Routledge.

Rachman, A.W. (2022). *Psychoanalysis and Society's Neglect of Sexual Abuse of Children, Youth, and Adults: Reassessing Freud's Original Theory of Sexual Abuse Trauma*. London: Routledge.

Rachman, A.W. and Mattick, P. (2023). *Freud, Dora and the Confusion of Tongues*. London: Routledge.

Rachman, A.W. and Mucci, C. (2024a). *Ferenczi's Confusion of Tongues Theory of Trauma: A Relational Neurobiological Perspective*. London: Routledge.

Book Reviews

Sándor Ferenczi: The Psychotherapist of Tenderness and Passion. (1997).

"Arnold Rachman's book is impressive for the way he's traced the evolution of Ferenczi's from that of a young disciple of Freud to a mature and independent thinker who proved that psychoanalysis could be both mature and humane. For anyone who is interested in the future of psychoanalysis as a therapeutic tool and particularly in the idea of attentively listening to what the patient is actually saying, this is imperative reading."

Phyllis Grosskurth

"This is the first book giving a complete picture of one of the most original companions of Freud, Sándor Ferenczi, … who is one of the founders of contemporary psychoanalytic technique. This work, a decade-long endeavor, is based on extensive research using English, German, French, and Hungarian sources. The unique qualities of this book (high scientific caliber, easy reading style, inspiring practical ideas) make it necessary reading for anyone who wants to be up to date on the understanding of the contemporary lively struggle for a renewal of psychoanalysis's thinking and especially psychoanalytic practice."

André E. Haynal

"Dr. Rachman should be heartily congratulated for the absolutely superb job he has done in reestablishing Ferenczi's rightful place as a hero in the history of the psychodynamic movement."

Paul Roazen

Psychotherapy of Difficult Cases: Flexibility and Responsiveness in Contemporary Practice. (2003).

"Arnold Rachman has written a compelling account of his work with difficult therapeutic cases. Emphasizing the importance of empathy, flexibility, responsiveness, mutuality, and personal honesty in the therapist, Rachman combines a boldly experimental attitude with a humane and compassionate spirit. While aspects of his approach may be controversial for some, Rachman's book provides a fitting tribute to the pioneering spirit of Sándor Ferenczi."

Jeremy D. Safran

"Steeped in the tradition of Ferenczi, Arnold Rachman has written an outstanding account of his creative clinical work in the Psychotherapy of Difficult Cases."

Beatrice Beebe

"Arnold Rachman has written a valuable treatise on the multifaceted problems of working with difficult and traumatized cases that are often dismissed as unanalyzable or untreatable. His extension of Ferenczi's idea of mutual analysis in a leaderless group of analysts is both instructive and riveting.

Joseph Reppen

Analysis of the Incest Trauma: Retrieval, Recovery, Renewal. A.W. Rachman and S. Klett. (2015).

"Analysis of the Incest Trauma is an elegant, forceful narrative of an awakening. First is the realization within psychoanalytic theory and practice of the actuality of sexual transgressions within families. Second is the documentation, in compelling, jargon-free descriptions of successive case studies. The reader will emerge with an enhanced sensitivity to the skill and empathic understanding required for helping patients to feel safe in the face of retraumatization – a model beginning with Ferenczi.

Joseph D. Lichtenberg

"Arnold Rachman's work over the past three decades has greatly helped our field recognize the importance of childhood sexual trauma and Ferenczi's contributions. Using the original exchange of letters, the authors have given us a detailed historical account of the struggle between Ferenczi and Freud over the role of childhood sexual trauma and its place in the history of psychoanalysis."

Beatrice Beebe

"The authors have quite deftly managed to do something rare: write a book about complex and painful issues that is tonally perfect. Their approach uniquely pairs the clinical experience of analysis with the deep, non-intrusive empathy required when working with incest victims. With remarkable frankness, compassion, simplicity and intelligence, they allow us to accompany them on the very demanding journeys they undertook with their patients, leading us through not only the gratifying, at times almost miraculous episodes, but also through the rough, distressing, even almost hopeless hours. The humility and courage with which they share their experience commands respect. Truly, a wonderful book."

Michael Larivière

The Budapest School of Psychoanalysis: The Origin of a Two-Person Psychology and Empathic Perspective. (2016).

"This superb new collection ... on the legacy of Sándor Ferenczi is a major contribution to the growing field of Ferenczi scholarship and to our understanding of the history and seminal influence of the Budapest school of psychoanalysis. This is a must read for anyone interested in the history of psychoanalysis and concerned about its future."

Jeremy D. Safran

"Arnold Rachman's combination of scholarly knowledge and practical experience as a psychotherapist makes this book both intellectually exciting and emotionally resonant, an invaluable contribution to the history of psychoanalysis."

Paul Mattick

Elizabeth Severn: The "Evil Genius" of Psychoanalysis. (2018).

"With the typically courageous attitude of the pioneer, Arnold Rachman adds with this new volume another great piece in the puzzle of the reconstruction of the real story of psychoanalysis, not only what has been accepted but also what has remained unseen, unheard because silenced: the voice of Elizabeth Severn, one of the most important cases analyzed by Sándor Ferenczi in his Clinical Diary. This is a book that is going to change the history of psychoanalysis and of trauma theory, restituting the right place to unjustly marginalized women psychoanalysts."

Clara Mucci

"Rachman's wonderful book traces the hide and seek of the tale – the hiding of Elizabeth Severn's identity, her and Ferenczi's influence on the field, and her remarkable life and wisdom. Psychoanalysts, historians, and interested readers will all find much to learn and by intrigued by in his book."

Joseph D. Lichtenberg

"Arnold Rachman has been the heart and soul of the American psychoanalytic community working to rediscover Sándor Ferenczi. He has been a meticulous historian, archivist, and analyst of Ferenczi's work. This book tells the story of the interlocking work and life and clinical encounters of Ferenczi and his patient Elizabeth Severn. In reviving Ferenczi's reputation and work, he tells the story of Severn and mutual analysis as an inspired collaboration. In this volume we can trace the evolution of one of the crucial developments in psychoanalysis: the tole and potentiality of the analyst's transference, countertransference, and the inter-subjective space in which psychic change may emerge."

Adrienne E. Harris

Psychoanalysis and Society's Neglect of the Sexual Abuse of Children, Youth, and Adults. (2022).

"The publication of Arnold Rachman's book is a long overdue and necessary step toward correcting the record on psychoanalysis's neglect of childhood sexual trauma, its sequelae, and clinical treatment. He courageously draws our attention to topics psychoanalysis has turned away from, calling out the field's "death by silence" attack on dissenters and the damage explicitly done to the reputation of Sándor Ferenczi. This is a landmark book."

Ann D'Ercole

"For over three decades Arnold Rachman has been an important figure in the revival of interest in Sándor Ferenczi an the Budapest School of Psychoanalysis. In his latest volume, he fearlessly and methodically makes the case for an apology to the Ferenczian community."

Fergal Brady

Ferenczi's Confusion of Tongues Theory of Trauma: A Relational Neurobiological Perspective. A.W. Rachman and C. Mucci (2023).

"Rachman and Mucci take us into the origin and genius of Ferenczi's concept of the 'Confusion of Tongues', Ferenczi's insight into the trauma of child sexual abuse in the origins of psychopathology, and Freud's campaign against Ferenczi's ideas. The book is a rich, erudite, and close up view into Ferenczi's contributions and the intellectual climate of that era."

Beatrice Beebe

"Rachman and Mucci articulate a clinical view of trauma that resonates deeply with our contemporary world. Diverse case histories and explorations into literature add substance to this important volume."

Howard Steele

"This deep exploration of Ferenczi's classic paper, 'Confusion of Tongues', brings scholarship and understanding to this contribution to psychoanalysis to a new level of detail and specificity. A powerful addition to our appreciation of what Ferenczi has meant to psychoanalysis, and to the crucial role of trauma in character formation and development."

Adrienne Harris

Index

For Product Safety Concerns and Information please contact our EU
representative GPSR@taylorandfrancis.com
Taylor & Francis Verlag GmbH, Kaufingerstraße 24, 80331 München, Germany